Praise for The 7 Principles of Conflict Resolution

'Clear, open, honest and direct communication is the only way to address conflict, and this book is essential reading. Highly recommended!'

Dr Ivan Misner, Founder, BNI; *New York Times* bestselling author

'If we consider conflict simply as a state of being stuck, mediation is the art and science of becoming unstuck. This means designing an expansive, informal problem-solving conversation that is facilitated by someone who is outside the problem. Louisa Weinstein has written a wonderful handbook that focuses on building our mediative capacities and skills. It has something in it for everyone: mediators, lawyers and people in conflict. The case studies alone are worth the price. Read it, and you will come away with fresh skills and a renewed belief in the possibility of peacemaking.'

Kenneth Cloke, author, *The Dance of Opposites: Explorations in Mediation, Dialogue and Conflict Resolution Systems Design*

'Will prove to be an invaluable resource for both employees and employers. Conflict resolution processes are explained clearly, backed up by relevant and relatable case studies. A copy of this book should be available in every workplace!'

Alastair Wilson, Chief Executive, School for Social Entrepreneurs

'The book provides an invaluable toolkit to not only develop any director or professional's formal conflict resolution skillset, but also to strengthen personal skills in dealing with the day to day conflicts of our workplaces.'

Sinead Brophy, Managing Director, MSB

THE 7 PRINCIPLES OF CONFLICT RESOLUTION

PEARSON EDUCATION LIMITED
KAO Two
KAO Park
Harlow
CM17 9NA
United Kingdom
Tel: +44 (0)1279 623623
Web: www.pearson.com/uk

First edition published 2018 (print and electronic)

The Financial Times. With a worldwide network of highly respected journalists, *The Financial Times* provides global business news, insightful opinion and expert analysis of business, finance and politics. With over 500 journalists reporting from 50 countries worldwide, our in-depth coverage of international news is objectively reported and analysed from an independent, global perspective. To find out more, visit www.ft.com/pearsonoffer.

ISBN: 978-1-292-22092-5 (print)
         978-1-292-22093-2 (PDF)
         978-1-292-22094-9 (ePub)

British Library Cataloguing-in-Publication Data
A catalogue record for the print edition is available from the British Library

Library of Congress Cataloging-in-Publication Data
A catalog record for the print edition is available from the Library of Congress

10 9 8 7 6 5 4 3 2 1
23 22 21 20 19

Front cover image © FaberrInk/iStock/Getty Images Plus

Print edition typeset in 9.5/14, Stone Serif ITC Pro Medium by Aptara
Printed by Ashford Colour Press Ltd, Gosport

NOTE THAT ANY PAGE CROSS REFERENCES REFER TO THE PRINT EDITION

THE 7 PRINCIPLES OF CONFLICT RESOLUTION

Pearson

At Pearson, we believe in learning – all kinds of learning for all kinds of people. Whether it's at home, in the classroom or in the workplace, learning is the key to improving our life chances.

That's why we're working with leading authors to bring you the latest thinking and best practices, so you can get better at the things that are important to you. You can learn on the page or on the move, and with content that's always crafted to help you understand quickly and apply what you've learned.

If you want to upgrade your personal skills or accelerate your career, become a more effective leader or more powerful communicator, discover new opportunities or simply find more inspiration, we can help you make progress in your work and life.

Every day our work helps learning flourish, and wherever learning flourishes, so do people.

To learn more, please visit us at **www.pearson.com/uk**

The Financial Times

With a worldwide network of highly respected journalists, *The Financial Times* provides global business news, insightful opinion and expert analysis of business, finance and politics. With over 500 journalists reporting from 50 countries worldwide, our in-depth coverage of international news is objectively reported and analysed from an independent, global perspective.

To find out more, visit **www.ft.com**

THE 7 PRINCIPLES OF CONFLICT RESOLUTION

How to resolve disputes, defuse difficult situations and reach agreement

LOUISA WEINSTEIN

 Pearson

Harlow, England • London • New York • Boston • San Francisco • Toronto • Sydney
Dubai • Singapore • Hong Kong • Tokyo • Seoul • Taipei • New Delhi
Cape Town • São Paulo • Mexico City • Madrid • Amsterdam • Munich • Paris • Milan

PEARSON EDUCATION LIMITED
KAO Two
KAO Park
Harlow
CM17 9NA
United Kingdom
Tel: +44 (0)1279 623623
Web: www.pearson.com/uk

First edition published 2018 (print and electronic)

The Financial Times. With a worldwide network of highly respected journalists, *The Financial Times* provides global business news, insightful opinion and expert analysis of business, finance and politics. With over 500 journalists reporting from 50 countries worldwide, our in-depth coverage of international news is objectively reported and analysed from an independent, global perspective. To find out more, visit www.ft.com/pearsonoffer.

ISBN: 978-1-292-22092-5 (print)
          978-1-292-22093-2 (PDF)
          978-1-292-22094-9 (ePub)

British Library Cataloguing-in-Publication Data
A catalogue record for the print edition is available from the British Library

Library of Congress Cataloging-in-Publication Data
A catalog record for the print edition is available from the Library of Congress

10 9 8 7 6 5 4 3 2 1
23 22 21 20 19

Front cover image © FaberrInk/iStock/Getty Images Plus

Print edition typeset in 9.5/14, Stone Serif ITC Pro Medium by Aptara
Printed by Ashford Colour Press Ltd, Gosport

NOTE THAT ANY PAGE CROSS REFERENCES REFER TO THE PRINT EDITION

CONTENTS

ABOUT THE AUTHOR

Louisa has been passionate about mediation and dispute resolution since practising law over 20 years ago where she saw how mediation provided solutions
where the law fell short.

She is driven by the possibilities for innovation in the field of conflict resolution. Fifteen years of mediation experience has showed her that mediation
doesn't have to be inevitable, just as litigation is no longer the only solution
today. Professionals and individuals can be taught how to do it for themselves
and their organisations. In this way conflict and its resolution can become a
force for change and growth.

Louisa's passion for advancement in resolution culture does not stop at the
corporate door. Children and young adults face increasing exposure to conflict
whatever their background. Louisa has designed and delivered specific
training and work experience programmes for young people teaching personal
conflict coaching skills to build resilience, thrive through online and offline
conflict and break glass ceilings.

Louisa heads up The Conflict Resolution Centre bringing together a team of
exceptional mediators and trainers serving clients across various sectors
(media, property, IT, technology, professional services, financial services,
charities) covering a range of issues including corporate and commercial,
employment, workplace, property, inheritance, personal injury and intellec-
tual property. Louisa is also an Associate Tenant at Doughty Street Chambers.
She is married with two daughters who are her perpetual and constant
teachers.

INTRODUCTION

What this book will do for you

The principal mission of this book is to support you and the people around you to start thriving in the midst of the conflict situations you encounter in your day-to-day life and avoid them resulting in business and relationship breakdown and court.

Specifically, *The 7 Principles of Conflict Resolution* will support you to get what you want and need to transform the range of conflict situations that most of us encounter during our professional and personal lives into situations that serve us.

Conflict can be simply described as the enduring condition where I disagree with you. When we see it in this way it becomes easier to accept its existence and find a way through it as a fact of life. When we think about it, we realise that 'justice' in any given situation will mean something slightly different to each of us. When you break down the component parts of conflict, you can start to see how it arises, how it affects us and how it subsequently affects us. As a result you become more able to manage and take control of it more effectively in your life, your organisation or your community.

During the course of the book we will discuss how conflict comes about and starts to cause problems, and where the Seven Principles can be most effective. Broadly, when I talk about conflict I will be concentrating on situations where communication is difficult or broken and specifically situations where I disagree with you, or vice versa. The type of scenarios this will apply to may range from difficult conversations and negotiations to entrenched disputes of word and pen and ultimately legal battles.

What we will not cover specifically is marital breakdowns and subsequent divorce or family mediation, although the principles will be useful in these situations.

As much as possible the information provided in this book will apply internationally. However, particularly with respect to organisational and court processes, you may need to find out more about the requirements and practices of specific jurisdictions.

The focus of this book will remain firmly on finding a solution or end to the problem that the individual or individuals will be able to live with going forward. Often the test of whether a conflict has been resolved will be whether it still keeps you up at night or whether the resolution is sustainable. Whether a conflict has been resolved will always depend on the individuals involved and can include:

● arriving at a formal or informal agreement

● receiving an apology

● agreement on a way forward to rebuild a relationship

● being able to let go of resentments

● the end of an argument.

Ultimately, the aim of this book is to help individuals and conflict resolution practitioners to achieve successful results in difficult circumstances without compromising reputation, dignity or self-respect.

Often in such situations conflict can follow a typical life cycle. This book will explain each stage of that life cycle so you know what to do when. By providing tools for situations ranging from difficult conversations and negotiations to entrenched deadlock, you should achieve the best results at all stages.

Crucially, it allows you to negotiate positive outcomes and avoid the personal and commercial consequences of destructive relationship breakdown, where possible, without the need to go to court or litigation.

Through *The 7 Principles of Conflict Resolution*, you will be given a comprehensive route-map to be more successful personally and professionally. The three parts of the book serve as building blocks to resolution, whatever stage you find yourself at.

Part 1 helps you understand how conflict arises and the fundamentals of what it takes to resolve it. Through that understanding, you will become better prepared to deal with it. Specifically, this part will equip you with the mindset that will be key to resolving most conflict situations by taking you through the theory of conflict resolution. This will provide a strong foundation to enable you to employ the skills set out in Part 2.

Part 2 takes you through the skills and tools you will need to address and resolve conflict and build on your mindset. In particular, it will support you through the process of modifying your approach to difficult conversations and negotiations and enable those around you to do the same.

Finally, **Part 3** enables you to make the best use of mediation (should you need it) as a tool in the conflict resolution process. It acknowledges mediation not as a signal that early resolution has failed, but as the appropriate solution in certain, often complex, circumstances. It allows you to be in charge of that process and be equipped to use it effectively as opposed to being victim to it.

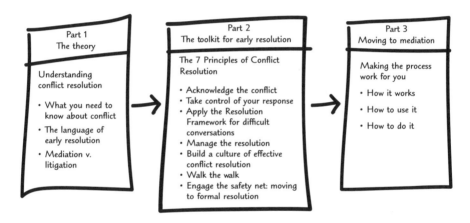

The focus, throughout will be to provide you with tools and strategic solutions which sit behind the Seven Principles to:

- develop clear, structured negotiation strategies with clients, colleagues, partners and other 'adversaries' to proactively deal with differences of opinion
- lead and coach others through difficult conversations and negotiations
- develop existing mediation and negotiation skills
- become more effective at managing your own behaviours, emotions and actions in highly charged situations
- explore and test new mediation and conflict coaching skills
- manage a diverse workforce by better understanding their various communication styles

- turn around entrenched positions and relationships to enable conversation and resolution
- create a resolution-focused culture in the workplace
- use mediation as an effective alternative to court or tribunal.

What this book will do for the people around you

Often, in disagreements or conflict situations, we want the other person to change. We focus on how and why they should change and how to make them change. Often this creates more aggravation and upset and can even make the situation worse.

By practising the principles and using the tools carefully and patiently, you will find that other people will start responding differently to you and the situation will start to change. So, instead of being frustrated that the other person or people will not change, you will start to be able to transform the situation through your own actions and give others the opportunity to do the same without compromising integrity, values or principles.

PART 1
THE THEORY: UNDERSTANDING CONFLICT RESOLUTION

CHAPTER 1
WHAT YOU NEED TO KNOW ABOUT CONFLICT

Critical to understanding and resolving conflict is the need to become comfortable with it as something that we might often encounter and that we can always overcome. We don't have to like it to become comfortable with it. Rather, we need to reconcile ourselves with its existence. As uncomfortable as it may be, we need to find a way to acknowledge and accept that we are in a conflict situation. This doesn't mean that we can't set boundaries to ensure we are safe within it. Rather, that we let it exist within the context of those boundaries.

When we seek to suppress or deny conflict, the simple fact is that it escalates in the same way as putting a lid on a boiling pan. When we accept that conflict exists, start to become comfortable with it and stop shaming ourselves and others for it, we become more realistic about the situation and so more able to deal with it. With that more realistic, albeit rather more uncomfortable, perspective, we start to be in a position to address the issues at hand more practically and less explosively.

Fear and its antidote – play

Neuroscientists, such as Jaan Panskep, have identified that human beings are driven by seven ancient instincts, or 'primary-process affective systems'. These are seeking, anger, fear, panic, care, pleasure/lust and play.

'Seeking' is the instinct that moves us to explore our environment to meet our needs and is considered by some to be the most powerful instinct. It is what gets us out of bed in the morning, drives us to have our coffee and breakfast and choose what we are going to wear. This is the instinct that leads us to forage, explore, exercise our curiosity, expect an outcome and feel euphoric by virtue of the search as opposed to the result that we achieve.

So, keeping the seeking instinct alive in a conflict situation can be crucial to achieving viable and creative options in negotiations. It also stimulates the dopamine that energises and provides the motivation for the successful conclusion of those negotiations.

The seeking instinct can be shut down when the fear and panic instincts take over. These two instincts can be triggered through all kinds of arguments: with a business partner, the withdrawal of an investment opportunity, a mistake that endangers business growth, a management or performance issue putting a manager and direct reports at odds or a neighbourhood or freeholder disagreement that can affect a home, financial, and in some cases, emotional security. It can be triggered not only by a professional adviser who is concerned about the chances of their client winning a case, but also their legal and commercial team who will necessarily experience consequences in the face of actual or potential loss. It can also be very contagious and difficult to shake off when it takes hold.

Scientists tell us that when we are in fear or panic mode we are experiencing actual or potential loss of social disenfranchisement, and so our ability to connect and, specifically, negotiate with others becomes compromised. Our ability to seek is also dulled and with it our ability to go through the process that takes us to a solution. So, even if we don't want to build relationships with the other person but simply get a good deal, our performance is being compromised.

When we are in conflict, the way we speak and hear each other needs to move out of fear/panic and into seeking, as it is there that we will find a resolution. One of the ways that this has been proven to be possible is through play. This is because play is vital for humans and other animals to build and test relationships. It may feel strange to apply the word play to serious commercial, workplace or deeply troubling personal situations until we think about what play would mean in practical terms.

Play in this context means being in a state where we can be creative and where we are prepared to get things wrong – playing with ideas without having a solution. In a game of tennis it would be the difference between playing to win and having a knockabout for fun. When we play we take the pressure of needing to achieve something off ourselves. This can feel frightening or uncomfortable as it creates what can feel like a void.

In fact, we are more prone to, and therefore comfortable with, filling that void with the stories, anxiety or drama we place around the situation than experiencing it. However, the void is critical as it creates the space for something new – a new idea, solution or perspective to come in. We start to focus on what is in front of us in the present moment and it is this that creates a different result.

Humanity has advanced, when it has advanced, not because it has been sober, responsible, and cautious, but because it has been playful, rebellious, and immature.

Tom Robbins

We are in conflict most of the time

Conflict is a very big word that most of us do not want to apply to ourselves. However, accepting we are in it is the key to unlocking the problems it presents.

Conflict is essentially an argument or disagreement that can arise between groups, individuals or countries. This argument or disagreement can range from being an obvious verbal or physical event or set of events but can equally start off as appearing relatively insignificant. Often the seed of the argument or disagreement will be a resentment or minor but persistent irritation that is ignored or not communicated – and then subsequently mushrooms.

Conflict can include all of the following:

- disagreement between politicians and civilians
- differences of opinion between manager and employee
- neighbourhood arguments about noise or boundary walls
- disagreements over strategic direction between board members
- arguments between children and parents over behaviour or boundaries
- disagreements about the use or otherwise of weapons.

It is important to distinguish between the conflict that exists and the consequences of that conflict including:

- civil war or unrest
- acts of violence
- depression, anxiety and mental illness
- business loss or breakdown

- relationship breakdown
- communication breakdown.

Failing to accept or address conflict does not generally make it go away but rather changes its nature and impact. This generally leads to an escalating of the conflict far beyond what it started as or was envisaged as.

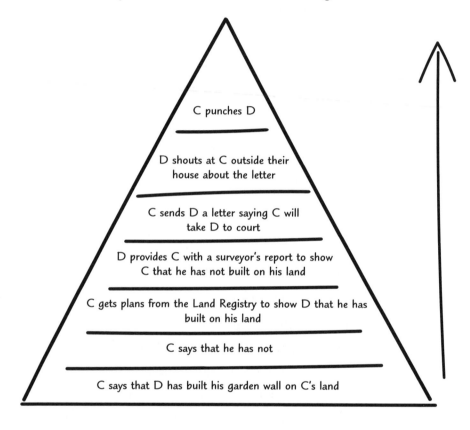

Whether a disagreement or argument is taken seriously is largely subjective and factors at play will include:

- how long the argument or disagreement has been going on for
- how much time has been or will be spent on it
- how much money will be or has been spent on it
- the damage, physical, emotional or other that it causes, is seen to cause or could be caused.

An individual's personal experience of a conflict can very easily affect its course.

First, the speed with which misconceptions and perceptions are discussed and clarified can have a significant impact. If communication is weak and what people say or think becomes unclear, we start to make up what we think the other person thinks, feels or is doing. We may often be correct but equally we may miss the nuances of the true situation. When we then act on those assumptions, we can often aggravate the situation.

Case study

Carl thought that Donald was deliberately encroaching on Carl's land and viewed the act of moving his fence as an act of aggression. When Carl started to think on it, he began to examine Donald's behaviour as he had experienced it (Carl had heard Donald shouting at his wife once) and his physical build (Donald is a weightlifter and was formerly in the army) and started to imagine that Donald must be an aggressive individual in light of that 'evidence'.

Carl did not want to seem weak nor feel in danger so he shielded himself with his lawyers. In an altercation between the two, Carl hit Donald to make sure that he pre-empted Donald hitting him.

In fact, the boundary on which the fence had been moved was arguable and they could have gathered evidence and come to an agreement about where it was and how they were going to define it. The violent incident made the relationship between the two individuals significantly harder to resolve and changed the conflict from being one about a boundary, that could have been resolved, to something far more personal and traumatic due to the assault.

Second, we need to be conscious that conflicts we experience in our day-to-day life can trigger pain or trauma from the past. If we have not resolved such pain, we often unknowingly experience the feelings and reactions we had all over again. We can feel overwhelmed and sometimes out of control of our reactions in a way that seems disproportionate to the situation that presents itself.

Case study

Annabelle's father was chairman of a global bank. Annabelle worked very hard at school, achieved great results but as a child she was always told that children should be seen and not heard. She found herself feeling uncontrollably upset and angry when she was in situations where people talked over her. She was not aware that every time this happened in adulthood she was reacting to her father's attitude towards her and that these events triggered old feelings that actually had very little to do with her present reality. Once she became aware of her response and the reason behind it, she became more able to temper her reactions.

Creating new opportunities

Most of us are clear about the negative associations of conflict. However, we forget that the most powerful conflict resolution processes can transform the nature of the conflict itself into new opportunities. These are opportunities that would not have existed or been envisaged had it not been for the conflict. This is not just a matter of putting a positive spin on a difficult situation – it is knowing that difficult situations always contain the seed of potential opportunities if we are prepared to address the situation and actively seek the opportunity.

Case study

Jim was the highest performing trader at an investment bank. He worked very long hours and he was concerned about the impact that might have on his family life when his wife had a baby. He spoke to his boss regularly about reducing his hours and working partly from home so that he could cut down on travel time and spend more time with his family. His boss said that he wouldn't consider this and that this was 'not the way it worked in banking'.

Jim thought about the situation and said to his boss that if there was no flexibility he would have to leave. At first, he was worried that the decision was going to cost him everything, but he finally decided to go into business with a former client to develop a trading platform, which meant he could work from home. Also, the bank later asked him to return to consult with them on better staff retention and opportunities.

This case clearly illustrates the opportunity for conflict to:

- enable people to re-evaluate what they want and what they think
- force people to think creatively
- take calculated and necessary risks
- provide valuable feedback
- pro-actively challenge the status quo
- learn from mistakes.

Resolution and regaining control

It is easy to fall into disagreements with people and then find yourself in litigation. Sometimes these kinds of situations seem to come out of nowhere. We often refer to this as the 'suddenly syndrome' – suddenly everything went wrong – when there had actually been a build-up towards that point of very small issues that had accumulated over the course of time but had not been addressed.

Once the cycle of disagreement and blame starts, it can self-perpetuate quite easily as it takes on its own energy and feeds itself. We can even end up feeling out of control and victim to it.

To take the situation in a different direction requires a conscious choice. The choice can often feel like taking a shot in the dark and entering the unknown. Not many of us feel comfortable jumping into the unknown as there are many risks involved in making this choice. There's the risk that the matter will not be resolved despite the effort, the risk of being vulnerable and becoming more open to blame, the risk of being manipulated and the risk of compromising a more aggressive approach. This is often the reason why we allow disputes and disagreements to rage on for years because it feels like the safe option.

In making the choice to resolve the situation, we take back some, if not all, control over the situation, stopping it to some degree in its tracks. This decision may need to be taken more than once over the lifetime of the conflict and it may even result in a later decision to fight. However, in making the choice to resolve the situation and reviewing that choice, we keep our options – and the range of possible outcomes – open. In this way, we allow ourselves to be more conscious of the choices we are making and less likely to be carried along by, and victim to, the conflict.

CHAPTER 2
THE LANGUAGE OF EARLY CONFLICT RESOLUTION

The language we use in a conflict situation can determine the escalation (or otherwise) of that situation. It is the difference between 'We've got a real fight on our hands' and 'We need to look at how we can work this out'. In particular, the language we use will need to strike the balance between acknowledging the issue and turning the existence of the conflict itself into a problem, thereby transforming it into something bigger than it actually needs to be.

Timing can be everything in resolving a conflict. The earlier the conflict can be addressed, the more opportunities for resolution and creative solutions there are available. At the same time, early stage conflicts or disagreements can run their course so it is important to avoid escalating them into something bigger than they need to be.

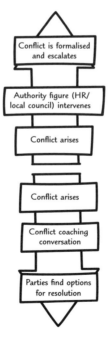

Personal conflict coaching

Although many of the early resolution tools and techniques discussed here are based on the principles of mediation, the essence of this book focusses around personal conflict coaching. This is the role individuals and managers can adopt to allow conflict to be addressed at an early stage. The personal conflict coaching set out in this book provides a unique, time-efficient and sustainable approach to ongoing conflicts and enables a sustainable culture of early resolution.

In our normal day to day, we are inclined to egg each other on when talking about conflict situations. If a friend or colleague complains to us about someone we often sympathise and agree with them, as opposed to helping them address the issues they are presenting. It is very easy for us to fall into the drama of the situation, and generally unknowingly, support the friend or colleague to be at odds with the other person and prove they are right and the other person is 'wrong' or 'bad'. We may decide that we also, as a result of the conversation, take issue with the other person – and so the conflict develops and grows.

A **personal conflict coach** (or conflict coach, the term we will use in this book) is someone who will serve as a support to an individual in a conflict situation and help them find a roadmap out of that situation. Their role will be to balance and ground the individual in that situation. The conflict coach will help avoid the dysfunctional blaming and shaming behaviour that we have established fuels the conflict by guiding the individual to work through that situation, take responsibility for the part they have to play in it and become empowered to take action or make decisions throughout the process. They will serve both as a coach and an impartial champion who will enable the other person to achieve solutions as opposed to become entrenched in their position.

When we talk about coaching in this context, we are not necessarily talking about being a qualified coach but rather about applying some of the thinking or assumptions that a coach might use. These ways of thinking or coaching assumptions can include:

- being supportive
- enabling conversations that are built on truth, openness and trust

- enabling others to take responsibility for their own lives
- believing in the abilities and potential of others
- not judging or giving advice.

When we talk about a coachee, we are simply referring to someone who is receiving this sort of informal coaching support.

In practical terms, a personal conflict coach could be a manager, a team member, a housing officer, a member of the local community, a fellow student and so on. How, when and where the conflict coach provides support will vary depending on the setting (community, workplace, campus).

Sometimes the conflict coach/coachee relationship will be very informal where one party asks the other to 'conflict coach' them through an issue. Having said that, boundaries will often need to be set up in the personal conflict coaching relationship. These will include the scope of the conflict coach's support, confidentiality and its limits, how the conflict coach and coachee interact with others, what happens if the conflict coaching relationship is unhelpful or doesn't work and compensation or "quid pro quo" for the conflict coach.

How this works will depend on the setting as well as the individuals involved. Organisations and communities using conflict coaches will also need to communicate that they are available, what their role is, how to access them and so on. Conflict coaches may be part of an organisation's early resolution scheme. These processes and practices are examined in more detail in Chapter 10 Principle 5: Build a culture of early resolution.

By adopting personal conflict coaching as a mindset, we are able to create an environment conducive to resolving our day-to-day conflicts. The result is that the focus of our workplaces and communities can move away from blame and shame and become less reliant on authoritarian figures telling us what to do. Rather, we move towards empowering, constructive environments in which we can learn and expand our horizons as a result of our disagreements and mistakes.

Facilitating vs fixing

In any personal conflict coaching situation, the conflict coach will never attempt to fix the situation. In other words, they will not try to resolve the situation or provide solutions. Rather they will facilitate the resolution process by enabling the individual with the presenting conflict to find a solution to it that works for them. The belief systems we bring to a situation can open up or shut down possibilities for resolution and are essential in creating or preventing early resolution.

In order to effectively resolve an issue we need to be conscious of the effect of not only our words but also the opinions, judgements and beliefs that sit behind them.

When we **facilitate,** we engage in helping others to work through a process or come to an agreement or solution while standing back and not getting directly involved in that agreement or solution. In other words, we help the process, agreement or solution to happen. In facilitating, we allow and even encourage a person to go through their process and find their solution. We do this in the belief and knowledge that the person presenting with an issue or a problem can find the answers to their challenges and problems because they know more about those challenges and problems than anyone else. The facilitator is just the agent to support the process of finding those answers.

When we **fix,** we present a solution to the problem to make it go away, and to some degree, to take away the problem from the other person. However, when we do this, we come from the perspective of our own limited beliefs or perspective and assume that we know the answer – or that there is no answer. Examples of limiting beliefs or perspectives are 'I know better than this person', 'They are never going to achieve what they think they can', 'They are not capable of xyz.'

We also generally come from a perspective of urgency – that something needs to be done about the situation now. Our feelings of urgency generally translate very quickly into fear or anger driven by the pressure of finding the 'right' solution. This risks shutting down the possibility of finding a true or sustainable solution because the range of what is possible or what could be true starts to diminish.

When we fix, we risk shutting down the seeking instinct and triggering the fear/panic instinct. This is because in fixing or telling somebody what they should do, we take the problem away from the individual experiencing it, and in so doing effectively tell them that they may not be capable of addressing the situation themselves.

Facilitating and playing with the issues may arrive at the same result as when someone tries to fix the situation. However, facilitating play allows the parties to explore the issue and open up the possibilities. It also has the potential to allow an honest and blame-free conversation that can get to the core of the issue, ensuring that it does not resurface as opposed to putting a plaster over it.

Expansive listening and questioning

For play or creativity to be possible, we need to make space for it through expansive listening and questioning. These are set out as steps 11 and 12 in Chapter 6 Principle 3: Applying the resolution framework for difficult conversations.

Many of our conflicts could be avoided if we practised deep or expansive listening with the other person. This means not just listening to the words and body language and the inferences of the other person but also being aware of what is not being said or being skipped over.

Expansive listening requires us to empathise and, as such, be prepared to suspend our judgemental nature. We cannot play if we feel judged. We need to be heard and feel safe in what we are talking about in order to play with or explore the solution.

The requirement to suspend our judgemental nature, in turn, requires us to acknowledge how judgemental we are on a day-to-day basis. During the course of one day, we can make judgements about whether we can trust people to be our friends, share a confidence or carry out a particular job, and in so doing we make decisions or judgements about what we think they are capable of, what their values are, what they think and so on.

If we start to notice the judgements that we are making about other people, even the most non-judgemental of us will realise that we do it all day long. You may right now be judging me while you are reading this book! Discernment and judgement are key to making good decisions but can potentially get in the way of expansive listening.

Just as expansive thinking enables us to open up opportunities, so expansive listening and questioning allows the other person to see the bigger picture and explore different perspectives, possibilities and options. Expansive listening and questioning does not limit the speaker with what the listener, or indeed the speaker, may think is possible at that time. Rather it allows for creative brainstorming which can often provide options for resolution that had not been previously considered or thought possible.

CHAPTER 3
MEDIATION: WHAT IT IS
AND WHY IT WORKS

Throughout this book, I refer to mediation even though most of the content will provide solutions that pre-empt the need for it. Why? Because the tools and principles used in the mediation process can equally be applied to situations in which the conflict has not escalated or when two parties are at loggerheads. It is the principles of mediation that enable resolution and that will form the basis of the seven principles.

The principles of mediation and why they matter

Mediation is a voluntary, confidential process in which an impartial third party supports the parties to come to a solution that works for them without giving advice or opinions. Between 70% and 90% of mediations are successfully concluded, indicating that it is an effective way to resolve disputes.

In a formal mediation, the appointed mediator will hold the principles as sacrosanct as they are the fundamental elements of the process that the two parties buy in to and take responsibility for. They are also the keys that establish the trust and independence of the mediator – crucial to support the parties as they reach an effective resolution. The mediator will be the guardian of these principals in the mediation process.

In informal mediation settings, using mediation principles are extremely helpful and the closer they are kept to, the more likely a meaningful resolution will be achieved. However, it is not always that easy to keep to them, partly due to other factors in play and partly to the experience of the informal mediator, conflict coach or 'resolution agent'.

The role and boundaries of the informal mediator, conflict coach or resolution agent and how they are managed is fully explained in Chapters 8 and 9 in

Principles 4 and 5. For example, when we informally mediate an issue between colleagues, we may feel an allegiance to the company and be concerned that we will feel or be compelled to disclose certain issues as opposed to being able to adhere to strict principles of confidentiality. Or an individual may feel that they are obliged to go to an informal mediation, as opposed to going to it voluntarily, as otherwise they may be seen to be obstructive.

Equally, the informal mediator may want to influence the parties to take a decision because they think it is the right one or one that represents their interests. It will be a balancing act that will require the informal mediator to apply the principles imperfectly and hopefully ask for help if they are struggling. Having said that, the principles adopted in formal mediation should be regarded by anyone in the middle of a dispute as standards to reach for and that achieve exceptional results.

The **voluntary** nature of the process means that it is necessary to come to the table and engage in the resolution process in some way. Whether that choice is because the individual feels that they have no other choice or whether they are choosing to take some constructive steps towards resolving the situation does not necessarily matter. Neither does that choice have to be a whole-hearted or happy one. The degree of commitment to that choice may, however, affect the quality of negotiations.

Often, when we do something because we have to, we can feel that we had no choice and therefore don't need to take responsibility for what happens. We move into a more child-like state of mind in which we subconsciously put the person who is making us do something in the role of punishing parent and we find ourselves acting out a child-like set of behaviours. Our level of commitment reduces as does our ability to drive the process and make good powerful decisions.

If I turn up at a mediation because somebody has forced me to, then I immediately feel a victim and my level of commitment to the outcome will probably be reduced. I am most likely to rebel against the process and the outcome as something that was not my choice. I will feel justified in my rebellion because I was coerced and may become disruptive as a way to take control of the situation.

It helps to look at the behaviour of young people in this type of situation as their behaviour can highlight in a more exaggerated way our more vulnerable and child-like instincts and reactions. We will explore this in Chapter 5 Principle 2: Take control of your response.

Case study

While writing this book I was working with a group of young people who had been identified as having child protection issues. Although they were pretty tough, they were also vulnerable. I was teaching them personal conflict coaching as a leadership skill. In particular, the course illustrated and modelled how they could become constructive leaders and that their experience could benefit others when they were able to turn the obstacles of conflict into opportunities.

We were considering their natural responses to conflict. During this process, I put the following scenario to them: A teacher puts you in detention unfairly for something you haven't done. Do you:

- do the detention anyway?
- not show up at the detention?
- show up at the detention but say you don't think it is fair?
- ask to speak to the teacher about why they put them in detention and to present the case?
- try to disrupt the class?

The overwhelming majority of the young people said that they would try to disrupt the class. When I asked them why, they said they had received the punishment anyway so they might as well commit the crime.

This illustrated very clearly to me that even though I may show up, as long as I feel forced or like a victim, or to some extent powerless, I will feel justified to act in a disruptive manner until such time as I choose to engage in the process.

Being volunteers in the process, we are already geared to make a series of choices and decisions that we can become empowered through. Choices will include:

- If I do not attempt to resolve this, what will I or the other person do next?
- What is important to me?
- What decisions do I need to make?

- Am I prepared to compromise?
- Am I prepared to think about compromising?

Even before the mediation, the process allows the individual to stop and think about the situation they are in and reawaken them to their choices. By requiring someone to volunteer to mediate (or decide not to), they are making a conscious decision about the way they want the situation to progress and, in so doing, put themselves back into the driving seat of that situation. The result is that they are also more likely to have to buy in to any decision or action resulting from that process and deliver solutions that may have not been previously thought of.

Confidentiality is probably the most powerful element in the mediation process and in resolving conflict generally. Specifically, this confidentiality will apply to individual conversations between the mediator and the individual parties.

To preserve confidentiality, the mediator must do the following:

- Explain and guarantee that they will not disclose any information that has been given to them in private meetings without individual authorisation from the parties.
- Double-check whether the parties feel comfortable that conversations with the mediator will be kept confidential.
- Obtain specific authorisation to disclose information if the party who owns the information decides that they want to disclose it.
- Ensure that only the exact information that the party agreed to disclose is actually disclosed – by writing that information down, reading it back and confirming again that it can be disclosed.
- Ensure that separate meeting rooms of all the parties are sound-proofed to the degree that each party cannot hear what is being said by the other.
- Set clear boundaries so that confidence is not broken by, for example, the mediator inferring certain information from one party that they have been told by the other party.
- Include a provision in the mediation agreement that is signed with the parties to keep confidentiality.
- Not disclose any information with respect to the mediation to third parties, in particular the names of parties or their companies if relevant.

Confidentiality provides an opportunity for communication to open up. It allows some freedom for people to say what they think to an independent third party without fear of it being disclosed or of being caught out by it. With the protective cover of confidentiality, individuals start to feel more comfortable about owning or taking responsibility for their part in what has happened without fear of being misunderstood or punished. They can also play with alternative scenarios without having to commit to anything, including amending their bottom-line position. In this way, the reality of what is happening or true, as opposed to the fear of what could happen, can be addressed.

In creating a confidential environment, sensitive information can be discussed and considered, as opposed to being covered up and ignored. It creates space for that information to be considered and strategies to be thought through to address the consequences of that information.

Case study

Jo and Sam went to university together and a few years later Sam asked Jo to invest in his business PROPCO and make some introductions to potential additional investors. They had agreed that Jo would earn a commission on any investment that the business received as a result of the introductions he made. Sam didn't pay Jo on one of these deals and Jo threatened to take Sam to court. Jo also suspected that there were other deals that he had entered into where Sam should have paid him a commission but hadn't. Jo also wanted to make sure that Sam would pay commissions to him in the future.

During confidential discussions between a mediator and Jo, it became clear that PROPCO was not making any money and was in danger of closing. Sam acknowledged to the mediator that he should indeed have paid commission on the deal as Jo had suspected but clarified that there had been no other undisclosed deals. However, he also told the mediator that he had some but not all the money he owed to Jo and could not pay him in full. Sam was trying to close a deal with one of the companies that Jo had introduced him to and if he did then he would be able to pay him. However, if that company knew what a precarious position the business was in, he was worried it would not invest.

During further confidential discussions between the mediator and Jo, Jo said that he did not want to take Sam to court and simply wanted to get his money back and know the truth.

Following the discussions with the mediator and having taken legal advice, Jo told Sam what he had told the mediator. The confidential discussion with the mediator gave Sam an opportunity to rethink the situation and work out what the risks and options were before presenting key information to Jo.

Although disclosing this truth was embarrassing and a potential risk for Sam, it allowed for a conversation that was rooted in reality. This in turn resulted in Sam and Jo agreeing a plan for Jo to help Sam close the deal with the investor and for Sam to be more open and clear with Jo about what was going on in the business.

Confidentiality was only one part of the reason that a resolution was reached but it was important. It allowed Sam to be honest and find a workable solution with Jo that could form the basis for them to work together for their mutual benefit.

Mediation is a process with a clear structure and the mediator is simply the vehicle to execute the process. This is important because making it about the process, rather than the mediator, keeps the focus on the parties and the issues. Often, we hand over all responsibility to advisers and then are disappointed in the result. The mediation process allows us to get back in the driving seat and use advisers to their best advantage without handing over our lives to them. This serves as a win–win for both client and adviser.

Key elements of the mediation process are set out in Part 3 of this book.

The requirement for an independent third party who does not give advice or opinions can seem counter-intuitive, but it is essential to obtaining a sustainable solution. The mediator will never know as much about the situation as the respective parties, or even their advisers, and therefore will never be able to see all the angles. By not limiting the process to what the mediator may or may not know, the following becomes possible:

- The solution is not limited by the mediator's knowledge or lack thereof.
- The mediator does not become invested in their own proposed solution.
- The mediator can focus on what might be possible.
- The parties can start to open up 'out-of-the-box' solutions without the limitations of complying or getting things right.
- The mediator can reflect back on the bigger picture including mutual priorities, interests and needs.

Litigation, mediation and other forms of alternative dispute resolution

Although this book focusses on mediation, it is one of a number of forms of what is known as 'alternative dispute resolution'. This is a term applied to forms of dispute resolution that serve as an alternative to litigation or, in other words, going to court. These will include arbitration, conciliation, mediation, negotiations between lawyers and simple face-to-face negotiation.

<u>Litigation</u>

Litigation is the action of bringing or being involved in a law suit. It covers situations in which one person takes the other to court, which will also include for the purposes of this book to a tribunal. The most effective use of litigation is in cases where a judgement absolutely needs to be reached with respect to a point of law. The action of starting litigation can be the trigger to explore and move to some of the alternative forms of dispute resolution.

If you are thinking about litigation you will need to:

- be clear about your case: who did what to whom and when
- be prepared to back up your case with evidence (letters, bank statements, contracts) as the stronger your written evidence, the stronger your case will be
- consider taking legal advice and engaging a lawyer
- be prepared to ask other people to get involved as witnesses
- establish whether you have any insurance in place that you can use to pursue or defend the case
- know how much money you have available to pursue or defend the case
- know that even if somebody did something you think was morally wrong, it may not be wrong in law
- think about alternative forms of resolving the dispute.

Litigation pros and cons	
Pros	**Cons**
Allows people to say that they are serious and that they are prepared to invest time and energy into fighting their claim.	There is no guarantee of winning at court. When pushed, the most experienced and expert lawyers will not, even in the most open and shut cases, predict odds of success at trial of more than 70:30 because you never quite know what will happen.
Clarifies the damage or compensation that people think that they are entitled to.	The costs of going to court can very often exceed the value of the claim itself. Often when costs incurred in fighting the claim are more than the value of the claim, people carry on through the court system in an attempt to recover the costs of fighting the claim in the first place.
Clarifies the positions held by both sides i.e. what they think and why.	
Provides an opportunity for people to set out their case including what has happened, what should have happened, why one party thinks that they are right and the other is wrong.	Litigation takes up substantial time to instruct advisers and review documents.
	Litigation can be disruptive and can lead to what is known as "Litigation Stress Syndrome". Even if individuals are not deeply affected by the process, for many it will increase their levels of day-to-day anxiety affecting sleep patterns, wellbeing and relationships with people who are close to us.
Provides a process to establish who is right and who is wrong in the eyes of the law.	
Highlights that there is a serious problem.	It may have an adverse effect on existing business relationships beyond the relationship being litigated.

If you are thinking about mediation before litigation, bear in mind that the other person will need to agree to go to mediation – the mediator will not make them go to mediation for you. You may want to take legal advice and carry out a mini risk-analysis with respect to the following:

- what your best and worst-case scenarios might be if you go to court
- what the likely cost of going to court may be

- how much time it might take to pursue the matter in court
- what your chances of success might be
- your top and bottom lines if you are to enter into an agreement
- how to make sure that the agreement at mediation is kept to e.g. a formal written agreement drafted by your lawyer.

Bear in mind that it is very unlikely that your lawyer will be able to give you a definitive answer with respect to these questions as things change. Even 'open and shut' cases can be complicated by new information. However, your adviser will help you to analyse the risks and benefits. Even if you do go ahead with litigation, these questions will be useful to return to and review during the process so that you are clear about the risks and benefits of decisions you make during the course of the court process.

Mediation is often proposed or suggested by the parties before litigation or when litigation is in progress. The threat of litigation can focus the parties' minds on resolution because of the risks involved and because it encourages an efficient timeframe. Current processes are geared towards winning and therefore escalating the conflict. This is because by continually trying to 'get one over' the other person we alienate ourselves from that person on a personal level and we become the opponent. Early intervention, including mediation, is an opportunity to stop the clock and climb off the conflict escalator.

Litigation, or the threat of it, is not necessary for mediation to happen. In fact, mediation can happen at any time and can take various forms from formal to informal. This is because it is a process that helps people to get whatever it is they want out of a conflict situation with another person. That might be money, justice as they understand it, an opportunity to rebuild a working or neighbourly relationship, or an agreement about ending a relationship. It is different from a court process that focusses on a decision being made that requires one person to be right and one person to be wrong on the basis of a set of core standards.

Both processes are important. Sometimes it is important for someone to be proven right or wrong and for wrongdoings to have consequences. Sometimes we need to define and construct our own sense of what justice looks like and create that justice.

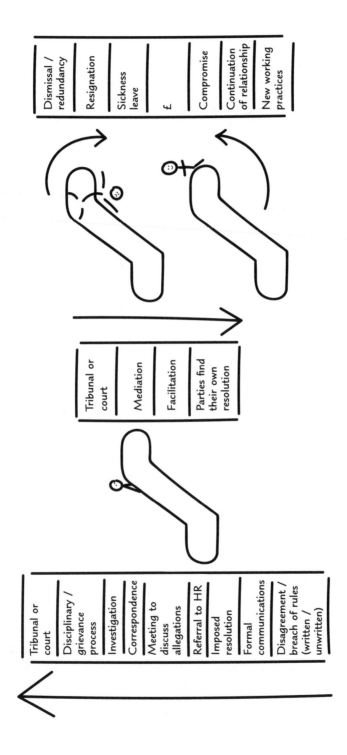

Arbitration

Arbitration is a process in which disputes can be resolved outside court and is less formal than court. Unlike a judge who will base their decisions on law, the arbitrator may take into account other factors allowing for a fuller discussion of the issues that may go beyond legal rights and wrongs. The arbitrator will, however, come to a decision or an award which the parties agree to be bound by.

Conciliation

Conciliation is similar to mediation although generally used only for employment disputes. The conciliator plays a similar role to the mediator but will be more likely to put forward a proposal for settlement – unlike mediation where the mediator is not involved in the process of settlement itself. Also, if the party has legal representation, the conciliator may liaise only with that representative and not with the individual.

Costs of dispute resolution

The costs of dispute resolution vary according to:

- when the process of resolution starts
- the value of the claim in question
- the complexity of the dispute
- the route taken to resolve the dispute
- where the dispute resolution takes place.

The table below sets down an example of the range of costs involved in dispute resolution in the UK.

	£5,000	£10,000	£100,000	£500,000+	1,000,000+
Conciliation					
Mediation					
Litigation					
Arbitration					

It is worth bearing in mind that the fees referred to in the litigation column above may also be incurred when going to conciliation, mediation or arbitration in addition to the cost of that intervention.

PART 2
THE PRACTICE:
THE 7 PRINCIPLES OF EARLY
CONFLICT RESOLUTION

Introduction

The 7 Principles for Early Conflict Resolution have been developed to provide you with a set of foundation skills and practical tools for approaching and addressing conflict situations when dealing with conflict in your own life or during the course of working with or advising others.

As a manager or leader, you will be equipped with skills to address challenges that you have with your staff and to better manage the tensions or blocks that they may be experiencing with each other.

As an employee, the principles will empower you to be more resourceful in dealing with conflicts and challenges at work, enabling you to better manage up as well as down and ensure your needs are being met.

For legal or professional advisers, the principles will enhance the value you add to your clients and increase your capacity to get your clients what they want and need and to achieve the best result possible in all circumstances.

If you experience conflict situations in your business, day-to-day life or community, the principles will give you opportunities to navigate through difficult situations with others and impact not only on their behaviour but also their experience of the situation. In all of these situations and more you will have the tools to turn around dysfunctional or negative dynamics, that you may have previously thought were hopeless, into a force for progress and change.

The one condition of this book working for you will depend on you keeping an open mind and not giving up too soon. An urban myth illustrates this very well.

There was once a man who was told that there was a pot of gold under his garden and if he searched for it he would find it. The man dug a number of tunnels under his garden over the course of many months until he finally stopped believing that the gold was there. The gold was later found by someone else an inch away from the end of the last tunnel the man had dug.

We have to know that even though we can't see a resolution it may be possible. The only way to see that is to keep practising the principles and honing your skills. In this way you will markedly improve your situation, albeit sometimes quickly and sometimes slowly, and you might very well come to find solutions or options that you hadn't considered before.

When and how you use the principles will depend largely on the situations you find yourself in and the change you want to effect. They start with supporting you to take responsibility and ensuring you are in the best possible position to achieve your goals. A developed use and understanding of the principles builds our capacity to support others without compromising ourselves and finally to being in a position to effect cultural change.

The principles can be used as standalone tools but are best used cumulatively. It is crucial to understand that part of our success in using the later principles to help others will be based on our ability to internalise and apply the early principles in our own experiences of conflict. Equally, sometimes we can take full responsibility and manage the early stages of conflict effectively but rely on people and forces other than ourselves to participate in that process to make the results sustainable. In these circumstances we will need to rely on the later principles.

The interdependence between personal and organisational application of the principles is set out in the virtuous circle below.

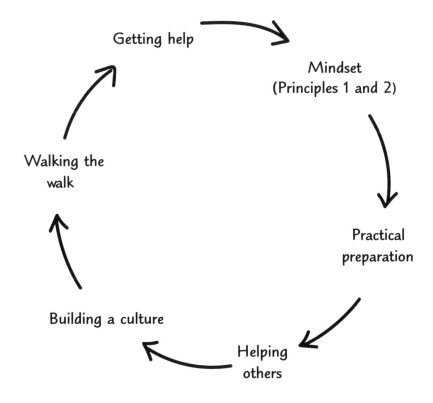

CHAPTER 4
PRINCIPLE 1: ACKNOWLEDGE THE CONFLICT

Conflict is generally not a word that most of us like to apply to ourselves. We may want to avoid making something out of nothing. We can fear that being in conflict with someone else means that we are not a nice person or that we are in some way weak. In reality, as we have established, what happens when we don't accept that we have a conflict situation can be that the conflict escalates or the behaviour of those involved deteriorates. This can be exemplified in a number of scenarios:

- Every day A asks B not to take A's milk at work. B ignores A and A puts a padlock on the fridge door. A and B are called in to see the supervisor.
- C is not satisfied with the quality of products delivered by D and does not pay D. D sues C for non-payment and C is unable to fulfil orders to C's clients.
- E gets upset with F, his upstairs neighbour, for making noise. E's son bangs on the ceiling when the neighbour makes the noise and when his father is out in an attempt to stand up for his father. F tries to talk to E about F banging on his ceiling. E says F is trying to wind him up and threatens to call the police to 'slap him with an ASBO'.

Case study

Jasmin worked at HomeHelp, a social enterprise focussed on helping people to be rehoused. HomeHelp was based in the offices of the local council and shared photocopying resources with council workers. Jasmin used the photocopier and when she came back there was a note on the photocopier saying 'Please refill the paper'. Jasmin was irritated that the person who had written it hadn't come to talk to her about it.

When she discussed it with her colleagues they inferred that people in the council didn't want them to be there and quoted a number of separate occurrences that backed up that belief. They went on to discuss the incident and further concluded that the council didn't respect their organisation. Further discussions unearthed that the person who had put the note on the photocopier was having an affair with the council's chief executive.

Although the situation started off with what seemed like a small irritation, it mushroomed into having far-reaching consequences. The fact that the communication was not working within the two organisations and that certain employees of HomeHelp felt that their work was not respected were valid issues. However, because these issues had been brought to light by something that seemed so petty, the conflict was not acknowledged. The result was that gossip was able to spread and opportunities for the two organisations to collaborate were missed.

When we do not acknowledge the conflict in the hope that it will go away, we risk losing control of our ability to manage the situation, as well as other people's responses to it.

Here are some **useful questions** to check whether you are helpfully acknowledging a conflict:

- Is this situation waking me up at night?
- Am I avoiding someone?
- Am I talking about someone behind their back?
- Am I avoiding talking about something?
- Is someone or something irritating me?
- Am I finding it hard to forget about something that happened in the past?
- Do I feel uncomfortable about this situation?
- Am I uncomfortable being around this person (or these people)?

If the answer to any of the above is yes, it may indicate that we are in a conflict situation. It does not mean that we have to run and talk to the person or deal with the situation straightaway. Rather, it is an indication that we need to accept that this is our current reality and work out what we want to do with that information. When we accept our reality, we often find that the fog of procrastination, worry, doubt, guilt or anxiety we experienced in not acknowledging the situation starts to lift and we are able to approach it with more clarity.

External conflict

When we think of the word conflict, it is rarely something that applies to us and more likely to be associated with war and political unrest. It is rarely a word that we apply to ourselves. However, it can start in lots of different ways including:

- Misunderstanding about what was expected or going to be delivered on a project.
- Verbal complaints from a neighbour about noise or security surveillance cameras.
- Non-payment of an invoice without explanation.
- Learning that someone has been talking about you at work.
- Someone else getting a bonus when you feel you have worked as hard.

Case study

When I was working with a group of young Asian girls following a series of Muslim extremist terrorist attacks, we talked about what conflict was for them. I was almost nervous about talking about the conflict with them and was concerned that talking about it may alienate them from me and the course. Even though the subject was at the core of what we were talking about, I had to acknowledge that part of me wanted to avoid it. Part of me thought that talking about it might make them feel like I was judging them or their beliefs. In other words, I made up stories in my head about what they might think I might be thinking and what might happen and almost started to believe those stories.

When we did start talking about the terrorist attacks and their repercussions on the girls, we began to address misconceptions and prejudices including our own. The conversation became easier because we started to acknowledge the more subtle conflicts that flowed from the situation.

One of the girls said that she had gone to play football with a group of friends and another group of kids had said they couldn't play. The other group went on to imply that she and her friends were like terrorists and would stab them at the first chance they got.

When talking about the situation, they felt that their experience was being listened to and validated. They felt heard and understood. Together, we realised that acknowledging the subtleties of the conflict meant they could move through it and move on from it. We could acknowledge that the girls felt victims of the terrorism. They also got to grips with their thoughts and feelings that some people blamed their culture and therefore them for events and actions that had nothing to do with them.

The next week, one of the girls told me that she had gone back to the football pitch with her friends and that they agreed with the other group that they would share the pitch by drawing an invisible line down it and playing on either side. When the girl kicked the ball over to the side occupied by the other group they started talking. The other group apologised for judging them and for being aggressive and ended up pumping up the ball that had crossed on to their side of the pitch.

By acknowledging that they were in a conflict situation and talking about and processing how they felt about it, the girls were able to take a step back. This meant that although the interactions were difficult they were not as overwhelming or charged as they could have been in the second meeting.

Instead of harbouring resentment towards the 'establishment' or a certain group, they could say: 'What the terrorists did has had an effect on us. Some people blame people with our religion for the terrorist acts. I do not have to hate them for that as my hatred will ultimately eat me up and impact my own view of the world as a hateful place. It is not OK for people to treat me badly because of my religion. I understand that they feel frightened in the same way that I feel frightened. These people may end up being my friends.'

Learning to face our conflicts head on requires the guts to address the problem and demands us to dig much deeper into who we are and who we want to be. It is a process of growing up. This is a challenging concept particularly when posed to people in responsible positions with 'grown-up jobs' responsible for millions or billions of pounds and thousands of employees.

Our conflicts can result from actual or perceived judgements or seemingly little things that we feel are silly but no matter how petty we think they are, they still remain triggers that will need to be addressed and/or acknowledged later on. Here are some examples:

- A sarcastic comment that can be construed as a dig or judgement.
- A throwaway remark about the holiday leave someone takes.
- Copying someone in on an email who hadn't been involved in the conversation.
- A raising of eyes when someone says that they were off sick.

Internal conflict

One of the reasons why we ignore or do not address the conflicts we are confronted with is that they highlight our need to address our internal conflicts. These can be issues or thoughts that many of us will go to any lengths to run away from. We will call them our 'internal conflicts'.

From an early age, many of us begin very quickly to do things because we are scared not to. This can put us immediately in conflict with ourselves and the world around us. By the age of ten most of us have been asked what, rather than who, we want to be when we grow up. Many of us have dreams of achieving certain things which can very quickly conflict, or appear to conflict with, what we or others think we are capable of, the reality of paying the bills, raising a family, looking after elderly relatives and so on.

When conflicts arise, it is often these internal conflicts that come to the surface and that drive our reactions. They are very often the things that no one wants to address for fear of the consequences. However, the key to the win–win is in working through these issues and finding a solution based on the reality of who we are rather than who we used to be or who we think we should be.

When we do not acknowledge and address our internal conflicts, we can be unaware of how they are driving us and can remain stuck in difficult jobs or relationships while time and money are spent on the equivalent of trying to fix a serious sprain with a plaster. When we understand what our internal conflict is and how it is driving us in our external conflict we can start to make better choices and take better actions about what we need with respect to the matter in hand.

Case study

Josh was a lawyer. From a very young age he was keen to get his family's approval. His grandfather, also a lawyer, used to say that he would be a great lawyer and regularly gave examples of Josh's negotiation skills. This relationship influenced his job choice at an early age. Josh spent one summer working in a placement his school set up for him in a dynamic digital marketing start-up. He really enjoyed it and was good at it but decided to continue in law because he felt that was expected of him.

This was the start of his internal conflict as he was constantly battling with pleasing his grandfather and pleasing himself, though he wasn't aware of it most of the time.

At his law firm, the partners said they saw a great deal of potential in Josh's abilities to develop relationships and bring in clients. The only problem was that as time went by, he wasn't performing well in the core elements of his job. He often made rookie mistakes in the documents he put together for clients and had a poor understanding of the detail of the law.

Josh had always worked hard but found the job very difficult and deep inside he felt he wasn't made for the job. He continued to make mistakes and kept on trying to talk to the senior partner he worked for about it. The partner seemed to become increasingly frustrated but avoided talking to Josh about it, blanked him and eventually called in HR to manage exit conversations. This process took three months, compromising Josh's happiness and self-esteem. He was popular and many of the team started talking about him not performing but also how out of order the firm was for the way they were leaving Josh out in the cold.

Josh eventually left and joined a new firm where a very similar sequence of events started to unfold. He was offered a position in business development as the partners found him to be very talented in this area. He turned down the position because at the back of his mind he had a nagging belief that his grandfather would have thought that business development was below him. As it turned out, he missed out on the chance to work with one of the most successful heads of business development in the field. Josh was then asked to leave.

He found himself out in the cold and feeling unemployable in his chosen profession. He cut contact with the partners he had worked for and many of his former colleagues. He was convinced they thought he was a loser. He had alienated all his contacts and although he was not fighting with them in reality, was in conflict with them in his mind.

Josh engaged in some personal conflict coaching. He realised he was angry with most people in his profession and was therefore blocked from building relationships, something that had previously been easy for him. This led him to some more formal coaching where he accepted that his talent was business development.

Once Josh arrived at these conclusions, his ability to rebuild relationships with old colleagues significantly improved. He found that people were drawn to him because he was clearly good at business development.

He realised that this process would have been much smoother if he had more easily accepted his conflicts with himself and others. This can be summarised as follows:

External conflict (conflict with others):

- The senior partner he was working with was not prepared or equipped to talk to him about the issues.

- Alienating himself from other people based on an assumption of what he thought they thought about him.

Internal conflict (conflict with oneself):

- Avoiding or denying his natural gifts in business development because he did not think that would be respected by his grandfather or other people.
- Avoiding or denying the challenges he had with his current job because of career decisions he made when very young.

Had Josh and his original employer acknowledged the conflict earlier, they may have shortened the process by finding a resolution through:

- accepting the realities of the situation and identifying next steps
- supporting Josh with coaching or mentoring to make a transition to a professional role he was happier in and more suited to.

CHAPTER 5
PRINCIPLE 2: TAKE CONTROL OF YOUR RESPONSE

This principle is most useful when you feel out of control – either of the situation or your response to it. In these situations it allows you to take control before reacting or to regain control when your initial reaction is leading you in an unhelpful direction. Essentially, it enables you to get back in the driving seat.

I should highlight that this is not about taking control of the other person but taking our control of our influence over what happens next.

Most of us have a gut reaction to a conflict situation. This reaction is likely to be fuelled by instinct and, by definition, will not be considered or thought through. More often than not, we react to the situation without thinking about it and later work out that we would have preferred to have responded differently. When we do this, we lose control of our ability to respond in the best way to the situation. We only work out in retrospect what we should have done. This principle helps us to put a virtual pause on events and our reactions to them and gives us the benefit of a thinking process which otherwise comes only in hindsight after the horse has bolted.

Conflict requires an often complex verbal, emotional and physical response that can take time to consider and construct. However, our body tells us to respond to our instinct which is often not thought through and reactive. If we are being chased with a knife then we are wise to follow this instinct but otherwise we need to take control by understanding the complexity of the situation, our emotions and the permutations of the possible responses to it.

When we take control, we simply think about the situation and how we feel about it and take some time to work through options and next steps. Taking control means putting ourselves in a position to take conscious choices. To do this, we need to accept in the first instance that our initial reaction is not necessarily the best response.

The aim of this principle is to gain the ability to stand above our conflicts, see the big picture as opposed to what feels important at the time, and avoid regrets about how we respond to conflict situations in our life.

This is not to say that we should beat ourselves up when we do react and it does not turn out well. We can learn much from our reactions to conflict, both good and bad. So, before exercising this principle, it is helpful to take a moment to think about situations where you have reacted (The reaction) to conflict (The conflict), the positive and negative effects of those reactions (Pros and cons), what responses or behaviours worked well (What worked) and what we might have done differently or could do differently in the future (Things to adapt/change).

The conflict	The reaction	Pros and cons	What worked	Things to adapt / change
e.g. I didn't do what my boss wanted me to do	Deny that I had done anything wrong and blame other people for not supporting me	Pro: Recognising that I needed support and asking for it Con: Not taking responsibility for my actions	Recognising at least to myself that I needed help	Be open to accepting and taking responsibility for my mistakes and their impact, listen to instructions more carefully, be open to asking for help at an earlier stage

Stop

The very first step in taking control of our responses is to stop. The action of stopping gives us a crucial opportunity to take a moment to consider the situation we find ourselves in and how we choose to respond to it. If we stop long enough to accept that this issue is an opportunity for us to develop and get to our next level in our career or life, then we immediately equip ourselves with a powerful engine to propel ourselves to achieve the best results.

When we take time to stop, we can start to understand the dynamics at play and how we and others are responding to them. Once we become more conscious of how we and others are responding, we start to become more capable of exercising choices about how we respond to others and choose more strategic and thoughtful responses.

Reset the conversation

When we are in a difficult situation with others, even when we are not happy with our initial response, we can regain control of the situation. One way is sending an email along the lines of the one set out below. Note that my commentary is in brackets.

RE: Our conversation earlier

Dear []

I have now had some time to think about our conversation earlier/yesterday/last week. [*Most people appreciate it when we have thought about a conversation as it indicates that it is important to us*]. I am not happy about how it went [*This sentence avoids assigning blame – we could be unhappy about our own behaviour, the other person's behaviour and the outcome, or something else. Saying we are not happy does not overdramatise the issue but rather simply says how we feel.*] and I would like to make sure we deal with the situation differently going forward. [*Again this does not assign blame but says I want things to be different.*] Can we put aside ten minutes to talk about it next Monday? If not then, when might work? [*This is respectful, asking someone to put aside time to talk about the issue. We make the process of setting up a conversation easy by letting them know when we are free. We also put a boundary around the time we want to spend. Lastly we also give them an opportunity to talk about it at a different time but make sure that they let us know when that is going to be so that the conversation happens.*]

Regards

Find the adult in the room

My experience of the corporate world, as aggressive and competitive as it and the people who work in it may be, nurtures a culture of non-responsibility. As we get on with our important jobs in our capacity as important and intelligent people, we not only lose sight of who we are, and our evolving talents, but we stop taking responsibility for our own self-care, whether that be emotional or physical. In turn, we lose sight of our impact on those around us.

On a practical level, this environment can often be said to look after its employees, which you would deem to be a good thing. Meeting rooms resemble hotel rooms with butlers and beautifully laid out teas and coffees with labels telling us that if we want for anything we should contact Patrick who laid out the room for us today. If it gets late dinner is provided or as a treat pizza is called in.

One of the roles of HR in many organisations is to look after its employees and managers. Employees and managers go to HR to complain about unfair treatment and to be provided with a solution. Managers equally go to HR to fix or get rid of the problem so that they can get on with the real job of making money. The dynamic created is one of an enabling parent (HR) who takes the problem away leaving the child (manager) to repeat the pattern in which someone else takes responsibility for the issues that come up in the manager's relationships with others ad infinitum. Equally, in this dynamic, the employee expects to be looked after by the organisation and so ends up blaming both the organisation and the manager/colleague when the interpersonal situation is not resolved to their satisfaction.

In our communities we are bound by the rules of socially acceptable behaviour as well as social standing. We make assumptions about being better than or worse than others. We make judgements about our neighbours based on whether they have partners, families, jobs, an education and a variety of other factors. We are quick to call people stupid because they don't play by the same rules as us – they park in the wrong place or have noisy children to cite just a couple of examples.

These perceptions and judgements infiltrate our interactions and the roles we adopt. We end up going to authority figures: tenants' association, housing officers or even the police. Inevitably, our relationships and control over them weaken as we hand over power to a third party, and the conflict escalates particularly when that third party does not do or achieve what we want them to.

In the book *Games People Play,* Eric Berne explains the concept of transactional analysis. He unpicks the ego states of parent, adult and child that we move through when interacting with others. Understanding these ego states can be key to taking control of our conflicts.

The most effective ego state when we are in conflict is that of the adult. If we are in this state during a conflict, we are able to be measured in our response and more able to see and respond to the big picture. However, we have a tendency to move in and out of this state when we feel under pressure. It becomes very easy to move into parent when we feel the need to control or avoid confrontation. When we are in this state we tend to try to take responsibility for the other person and so enable them to be less responsible for their own actions. When we do this, we start to feel more resentful of the other person's inaction, less respectful of their opinions and often overwhelmed feeling that we have overall responsibility for the situation. Or we can start to move into child when we feel that we need to be taken care of or when we feel someone else is taking responsibility in some way for our lives and our consequences. At the same time we start to resent that person or organisation that takes responsibility for us and very easily feel that we are victim to our employers and circumstances as we start to hand over the power or responsibility for our actions to them.

When we apply this to the work environment, we see that the dynamic described above very easily allows the employee, however senior, to fall into the state of child who is enabled not to take care of their primary needs. As such, they subtly and unknowingly become disempowered. When we apply it to a neighbourhood environment, we might start to see one neighbour complaining more vociferously whilst the other turns up the music.

When we want to resolve the conflict we have to choose to step out of that dynamic so that both parties are empowered. When we walk away from the comfort of the parent–child relationship we move into the unknown where we have to start taking control of and responsibility for our own behaviour and we acutely feel that we make and live by the consequences of the choices we make. This is not always comfortable because we may not have an immediate solution to the situation and therefore may need to stay with it for a while and wait to see what solutions come without necessarily forcing them.

Here are some **useful questions** to ask to take back control of your response and respond in an adult state:

- What do I need to do to STOP in this situation?
  - Can I go for a walk?
  - Can I take time out in a coffee shop?
  - Can I sit in a park?
  - Can I find a quiet space to breathe or meditate?
  - Can I call a friend and ask them how they are?
- Do I feel overwhelmed or out of control of myself or the situation?
- Am I focussing on what the other person needs to do but not looking at what I need to do?
- Am I trying to take the problem away from the other person?
- Am I comfortable with the way I am behaving?
- Am I taking care of my basic needs? Do I need to eat, sleep or rest?
- Is it possible that X didn't actually do the thing I am complaining about?

CHAPTER 6
PRINCIPLE 3: APPLY THE RESOLUTION FRAMEWORK FOR DIFFICULT CONVERSATIONS (STAGE 1)

Stage 1: Preparing for the conversation

The resolution framework is set out in two stages, the first focussing on preparing for the conversation and the second equipping you to have the conversation itself. Although it is tempting to go straight to the process of how to have the conversation itself, preparation can make every difference so I would urge you to give equal attention to both this chapter and the next.

Success is where opportunity and preparation meet

Bobby Unser

When we are about to have these conversations, we rarely plan. However, through a plan we give ourselves the opportunity to anticipate challenges, be more prepared to deal with them and feel confident in our approach. This section outlines the steps we can take in preparing to make difficult conversations substantially easier.

Step 1: Manage your physical and emotional response

Fight, flight or freeze?

One of the most effective tools for managing our physical and emotional response in a conflict situation is to know that we are guaranteed to have one. Whether we feel immediately physically threatened or we feel a threat to our survival in the business or to our self-esteem, the same physiological reaction is triggered preparing us for fight or flight – and may also trigger a response to freeze. This triggers the nervous system in the body to secrete hormones to address what our body perceives to be a physical threat.

In many ways conflict generates energy that we can, almost despite ourselves, quite enjoy and build on. It is this energy that can keep us in conflict situations and can keep those situations alive. Many people I have spoken to report that when they are tired they still manage to muster up the energy to verbally attack someone else and that, somehow, they feel better or more energised from the angry release (if somewhat guilty afterwards).

Set out below is an effective way of harnessing this same energy generated through the conflict situation and managing it to drive through to an effective solution.

The emotional reaction to fight or flight, particularly in individuals with higher levels of emotional reactivity, can range from anxiety which generally manifests itself internally, to aggression which is more likely to manifest itself externally. So, from the get-go, we need to be aware that on some level it is not just going to be our brains but also our bodies that we have to master to overcome the situation. If we can take increased control of our bodies they can support us in allowing our mind to critically and creatively evaluate and address the situation.

Capitalise on your feelings

A surprising amount of us shut down our awareness of what we are feeling, preferring to prioritise what we are thinking. We can fall into seeing feelings as a sign of weakness, but instead they give us vital information that can carry us through the situation.

Our bodies can give us clues to what we are feeling emotionally as those feelings are stored in our bodies. These clues will be important to our success in dealing with the presenting situation. This can be for several reasons, ranging from the negative effect that stress has on our ability for creative thought to the way others perceive us and our strengths and weaknesses. Equally, this will create a knock-on effect on our mental capacity and resilience. An enhanced awareness of our own emotions will then equip us to rise to the challenge and influence the manner in which others behave and respond to us.

The simple act of identifying what we are feeling physically can immediately move us closer to getting a handle on a more advantageous response to the situation which can otherwise feel out of control or unmanageable. The following provide an example of simple physical clues:

- **Fear and anxiety:** Tight muscles, cold hands or feet, fluttery or sickness in the stomach, shortness of breath, general feelings of weakness.
- **Anger and rage:** Clenched jaw, tightened fists, headache, stomach ache, sweaty palms, feeling hot, shaking or trembling, dizziness.
- **Stress:** Insomnia, headaches, trembling, muscle tension, backaches.
- **Worry/Anxiety:** Inability to concentrate, dizziness, dry mouth, erratic heart rate, high blood pressure.

Once we have raised our awareness of what is going on in our body we immediately move to being in a better position to regulate that reaction. There are strategies to do this ranging from meditation to physical exercise which are powerful long-term strategies to deal with conflict on a regular basis. However, if this is not a regular practice and time or space is in short supply, one simple way of doing this is through focussing on your breathing and bringing it back to a comfortable rhythm.

Another is to take a moment to close your eyes and imagine a ball of bright light at the top of your head. Then imagine in your mind's eye the ball dropping from the top of your head through your face and your body all the way to your feet.

Alternatively, you can ground yourself by focussing on your feet, the position of your body and your posture. The key is to find a way to ensure that you feel present and grounded in your body and mind. Although these actions may feel uncomfortable at first, it is worth trying them out and exploring other alternatives that might be available and that may work for you.

Here are some **useful questions** to help manage your emotions:

- What am I telling myself about myself with respect to this situation? Am I telling myself any of the following?:
  - This is a catastrophe.
  - I'm stupid.

- The other person is stupid.
- This is going to affect my career.
- I'm going to lose my job, home, spouse, friends?
- If I said any of those things about someone else, what might they feel?
- Can I replace what I am telling myself with more helpful affirmations?:
  - Replace 'This is a catastrophe' with 'I have made a mistake, mistakes happen and I can forgive myself.'
  - Replace 'I'm stupid' with 'I am OK, I am perfectly imperfect.'
  - Replace 'The other person is stupid' with 'I can acknowledge the strengths of the other person without agreeing with them.'
- What sensations are going on in my body?
- Am I experiencing any physical discomfort?
- Can I help myself alleviate any physical symptoms I am feeling?
- Do I need help identifying what I am feeling?
- Do I need support to work through this situation?

Step 2: Write down your initial fears, wants and needs

Taking this action means that you do not need to go and talk to anyone else about the conflict you are dealing with until you are absolutely clear on what you want to say and who you want to talk to. It may be that once you have completed this step you find that the conversations you thought you might need to have are no longer necessary and the step will define the direction of the next set of actions.

FEAR: False Evidence Appearing Real

Sometimes our fears are well grounded. If someone comes at us with a knife we are likely to feel frightened. However, more often than not, the fears that consume us centre around what we think might happen in the future or even what we think other people might think of us. Although those projections can appear very convincing, they more often than not are not true, do not happen and are far from being foregone conclusions. If we can clarify what these thoughts are, we are more likely than not to catch them before they spiral out of control and become self-fulfilling prophecies.

To clarify, the difference between what I want and what I need is that the things I need are vital to either me or the organisation and what I want is merely desirable. What I want can be anything from 'to win the pitch' to 'to prove him wrong'. What I need will be the things that are essential to look after myself in the situation. We may want to stay with a particular company but need to progress or increase our salary. When we end up getting an increase in salary by moving to a more senior position elsewhere, we may have achieved what we initially identified that we needed as opposed to wanted. We may also find out that having focussed on what we needed that becomes something we also want albeit we had not anticipated that to be the case.

A difficult truth for most of us is that what we need may not always necessarily be what we want, but can be what is more beneficial for us in the long term. The more honest we can be during this part of the process, the more options we can then open up for ourselves. We also need to know that even when we identify our wants and needs, they will not necessarily be definitive but will move us towards our priorities and therefore help us be clearer about the decisions we make.

Here are some questions to identify your fears:

- What is the worst that could happen?
- What does this situation say about me, my abilities, who I am as a person?
- What might other people be saying about me because of this situation?
- Have I been in a similar situation that did not go well? Do I think that the same thing will happen again?

Here are questions to health-check your own needs:

- Is my mental or physical health dependent on this?
- Is my financial security dependent on this?
- Are people close to me likely to be compromised or put in danger or harm's way?

- Is my job likely to be compromised?
- Is my happiness and wellbeing dependent on this?
- Will I experience serious injustice if I do not have this?

And here are questions to clarify what you really want:

- If I do not get this will I look bad?
- Do I think I deserve this?
- Do I think that this will make my life or the lives of those around me better?
- Do I feel that it would be unfair for me not to have this?

You may find it useful to write down your own current fears, wants and needs with respect to a challenging situation you are facing in order to clarify the priorities you want to focus on.

Fears	Wants	Needs

Step 3: Change perspectives and see the bigger picture

This step helps us to stop in our tracks and change the way we are thinking about a particular situation by becoming more conscious about our subconscious thoughts and motivations. When we do this, we have more choice and control about how we think about and react to the situations we find ourselves in.

Understand and acknowledge your limited mindset

If you look at the news today, you will come across some kind of conflict situation occurring around the world. Alongside the acts of war and aggression that we witness between and within countries, we are accustomed to random acts of violence and terrorism perpetrated by seemingly normal young men and women. Often, at the root of these acts can be a personal outlook on the world which carries a perceived justification for their actions. This justification may be rooted in a feeling of disempowerment, not feeling respected, feeling like the system is corrupt, wrong and against the individual, a very real feeling that life just isn't fair and a feeling of entitlement to something better.

Essentially, these boil down in varying degrees to a self-centred view of the world when we are in conflict with it. In other words, it comes often understandably from a difficulty in seeing anything other than our version of events.

Although better disguised and often dressed up in socially acceptable behaviour, a similar albeit watered down self-centred mindset can exist in the workplace and in our communities. This can happen when we don't get what we want – or there is a risk that will happen – and we experience actual or perceived unfairness. In simple terms, our thoughts and feelings start to dominate our perspective on the world and trigger us to be more consumed with our own interests, needs, worries and concerns.

We might become increasingly driven by disappointment and anger at not having what others have, or a sense of lack of fairness and of not being appreciated for what we bring to the table. Our pride may start to take over. We may start to be dominated by fear that we won't get what we want and need. Equally, the shame of feeling like this or wanting the things we want may drive some of us to focus on our thoughts and feelings rather than the bigger picture. The more self-justified we feel, the more our thoughts and feelings then fuel the narrative that we create around the situation and the misunderstandings and miscommunications that ensue.

In practical terms, we might feel that our bosses don't value or respect us. We can feel resentful at corporate bonuses when we are struggling to make ends meet. We can feel disgruntled at paying taxes. We can feel irritated that our employees are asking for pay rises when they aren't bringing enough to the table. At this stage we focus on our upset rather than what we might be able to do to turn the situation around. Although our upset may be valid, it can also be a distraction from addressing the matter in hand in our best interests. Crucially, when we fall into this thinking pattern, we limit our perception of what is and is not possible.

Notice the effect of your mindset on your perspective

Although our responses to these situations are not violent, they can become very disruptive, such as undermining bosses in the course of pub gossip, taking excessive sick days, criticising the organisation at the water cooler, resulting in a lack of commitment to the job and lack of communication with employees. In terms of damage, this translates into days lost, poor treatment of clients and a lack of loyalty. When we adopt this mindset we can start to feel unheard, undervalued and ready to jump ship for a better offer that can easily end up in a similar dynamic or situation.

On a personal level, these thoughts and feelings turn inwards on the individual experiencing these situations and in turn can result in depression and sickness. The disabling consequence of this are extensive both in work days and money lost (find out just how much by going to this website: http://www. hse.gov.uk/statistics/causdis/stress/), but more importantly, the misery that is felt by individuals and families and communities on a daily basis.

In the workplace, the immediate knock-on effect of sickness and depression generally translates into reduced performance and lower profits. In our day-to-day lives it can translate into divided communities, social unrest, one-off acts of aggression and often in individuals cutting themselves off or hiding away from their neighbours to avoid the challenges inherent in situations where we can't seem to resolve our differences.

The bottom line is that to resolve conflict we need to be prepared to take responsibility for our own behaviours and reactions. This requires us to accept on some level that we have created or invited the situation into our lives to a certain degree. The natural consequence of this understanding will be that something in us, in our mindset or in our behaviour, will have to change if we are to resolve the conflicts that we find ourselves in. The bad news is that this will probably not happen quickly although this book will help you to achieve some quick wins. If done properly, it may in fact be a lifelong process. The good news is that where we truly learn the lesson the conflict has presented us with, we will increase our capacity for personal and commercial success. We will also be in a position to positively affect the people and communities around us and our small actions can be the make or break in affecting social change.

When we reach these realisations, we may start to feel overwhelmed. We may overthink or even obsess about the situation, believing that thinking or obsessing about it will solve it. It won't. This is a tall order but the suggestion here is only to take the foot off the pedal for a few moments. If we can physically move away from the situation we immediately gain some perspective. If we can then do a small action for someone else that is inspiring or enjoyable, we can significantly turn the situation around. By taking our focus off the problem and preferably giving someone else some joy for a few minutes, we can regain perspective and at the same time put something more positive into our environment.

Case study

I am extremely lucky to have worked at home while my children were young. One day I received a text from a colleague saying we needed to talk. I texted back to ask if there was a problem. My colleague said there may be. I hadn't been paid by our mutual client and was not getting any responses from another colleague who I had found to be obstructive so I started to worry.

I took step 1 – I sat down and focussed on a project that really inspired me. I then went downstairs and tickled my 18-month-old that reduced her and me to fits of laughter. Within a few moments I had moved from a place of anger and fear to one where I was playful, light-hearted, happy and much better equipped to carry out the other steps set out here.

The more adept we are at being open to adjust our perspective on the situation, the sooner it is likely to change even if nothing changes in the other person. We can do this in various ways but critical is moving out of thinking about ourselves and our situation and being able to think about other people. Even by reminding ourselves that there is a bigger picture, we start to gain an amended perspective.

Here are some questions to help change perspective or see the bigger picture:

- Can I think of someone who is having a challenge with something right now?
- Is there something I can do to help them?
- Is there anyone who would appreciate a call from me right now to tell them that I appreciate, love or am thinking of them?
- What random act of kindness could I take in this moment?

Find something in the newspaper that you feel angry, sad or passionate about and take some action to help that situation (donate money, write a letter, join a campaign, take a moment to think or pray about that situation improving).

Step 4: Get your facts straight

It is important to be absolutely clear of the facts before entering into the conversation. You do not want to be fumbling about for information instead of focussing on the matter at hand. You also need to know what your options will be if the conversation goes wrong. It is useful to be clear about your position if you need to take a more formal route later down the line. This step helps you think through the presenting situation and gather the information to help you make informed decisions.

List the information you need to have the conversation

The information you need may be emails sent or received, notes relating to previous performance meetings, details of financial agreements, photographs, specific and relevant feedback that is important to share. Basically, any information you may need to rely on during the conversation.

_____

_____

_____

If you don't have the information, what do you need to do to get it?

_____

_____

_____

In what way could the conversation go wrong and what management, HR or other advice authorisation or support do you need to take to manage this risk?

_____

_____

_____

Here are some questions to help you get your facts straight:

- What are the five key points you want to get across to the other person?
- What information would best help the other person to see your point of view?
- Do other people have information that contradicts what you are saying?
- Could the other people involved have information that compromises you or your point of view?
- Is it possible that additional information may clarify or resolve the situation?

Step 5: Identify and think through outcomes and options

A difficult conversation is, as much as anything, an opportunity to reset a situation. Like anything, if we can be clear about where we want to get to we are more likely to get there. When we identify our intended outcomes, and those of the other party, we not only build a vision of how we would like things to be but also where there may be room for alternative solutions and negotiation. The following set of questions will help this process.

What do you want? What are the best and worst-case scenarios of what you would like to achieve from the conversation? This will elaborate on your answer in Step 2.

_____

_____

_____

What does that look like? What is the detail of what that looks like and how would it work in practice?

_____

_____

_____

How far are you away from achieving that? What are the milestones that will be required to achieve your desired outcome?

_____

_____

_____

What are you going to do when you get there? What will the next steps be?

_____

_____

_____

What issues might cause you to change your mind, such as new or clarified information or a change of heart?

_____

_____

_____

Step 6: Clarify top and bottom lines

Any difficult conversation will include a negotiation, and in any negotiation it is helpful to know the boundaries before we go in. Our bottom line can be explained as the very least we would agree on and our top line would be our best-case scenario. However, once we have established our bottom and top lines, we may find that there is some room for movement around both as new information or circumstances come to the surface. If we can work out what this room for movement might be before we go to the negotiation table, or have the difficult conversation, we can feel a little more confident about acting in our best interests during the process.

The following questions should help you identify your best and worst-case scenarios and room for movement.

What is your ideal best-case scenario? Be ambitious – include everything.

_____

_____

_____

Which areas are you unable to compromise on? (e.g. If you lie I can't work with you.)

_____

_____

_____

Where, if at all, do you think you might be willing to compromise on what you want?

_____

_____

_____

Which areas, if any, do you feel unable to compromise on?

_____

_____

_____

What do you think the other person might want from the relationship or conversation? Base this as far as possible on what you know rather than what you presume.

_____

_____

_____

Where, if at all, do you think the other person may be willing to compromise?

_____

_____

_____

Step 7: Clarify your agenda

An agenda provides a framework for the meeting. It does not have to be formal but it can help to define your own and other people's expectations of the meeting, prioritise those issues and allocate enough time to address them. The agenda doesn't have to be formal, rather a list of key issues. You can send an email beforehand along these lines:

```
'I thought it would be helpful to let you have an overview
of what I am hoping to talk about at our meeting. I
understand that other things may come up on the day but
let me know if there is anything you would like to add
to this list.'
```

Then list the key issues you want to discuss in order of priority.

Try to put these in as positive and forward-thinking a light as possible – how you would like things to be rather than what is not working.

_____

_____

_____

If someone else is calling the meeting (and you are not sure of their agenda), list any issues that you think need to be addressed between you and that other person. Make sure that you do not raise them until you have fully heard what the other person has to say and what their agenda is.

Convert your key issues set out above into agenda items.

Issue	Agenda item
I don't want to meet with you in the first place because you talk over me and don't listen to me	Ground rules for the meeting
I can't work like this any more	Expectations for future working
You need to understand my perspective	Understanding each other's perspectives on what has happened so far
You need to behave differently	Boundaries for mutual respect
You need to talk to me differently	Communication
You need to tell me what is going on and not just expect me to know	Scheduling updates
We need a project plan for X Project and I should be leading on that	Way forward for X Project
I don't think we will have time to discuss everything	Meeting timings and follow ups

It might help to talk through with a colleague or friend how to convert an issue into an agenda item. When you do this, remember that the most helpful agenda items are impartial, open (create room for a discussion), focussed to specific topics, honest and do not assign blame.

It may also be helpful to allocate time to each item, but if you do add a note to your email saying something like:

> 'I know our meeting is set for [an hour] so to make best use of our time, I have suggested timings for discussion of each area in the proposed agenda. I have also allowed time for us to talk about a follow-up meeting in case we run out of time. Let me know if you have any adjustments.'

You will need to take account of the fact that some items may need more or less time than others (or than expected) so it is helpful to be flexible and to suggest to the other person that they should be as well.

Step 8: Practise empathy

When we are in conflict with others, we generally concentrate on what we are feeling rather than on what the other person is feeling. We often do not want to empathise with the other person for fear that our needs get lost. 'Why do I want to worry about how they feel, they should be thinking about how I feel.' Equally, we will be wary of seeming as if we are giving in.

There is no doubt that we need to address our own needs first in these situations in much the same way as we need to tend to our own oxygen on our aeroplane before helping others. This means that we have to acknowledge our emotions and crucially work out how best to look after ourselves in the presenting situation. If we expect the other person to be taking care of us in a situation of conflict and stress, we are likely to be disappointed and to set ourselves up for resentment which will further escalate the conflict. Just as we will be finding it difficult to empathise with the other person, it is unwise to assume that they will find it easy to do the same with us.

If we can do it, empathising with the other person will give us a great advantage over the situation. It will give us access to information about them and their response to the situation and move us out of our childlike self-seeking state. The effect on us will be that we will feel more grounded and more in control. It may also enable us to see more areas of commonality than we originally imagined which, in turn, may unearth solutions. Crucially, it will help us to feel happier about the situation and ourselves.

When we have the incentive that empathy may help us to achieve our goals, it becomes easier to practise, as does breaking down what it means and what we can do to achieve it in situations where we may not naturally feel it. Brenee Brown describes empathy immaculately in her RSA short on Empathy versus Sympathy which I recommend you watch (www.youtube.com/watch?v=1Evwgu369Jw). She explains that there are a few things we can focus on to train ourselves to practise empathy:

- Perspective-taking – accepting and respecting another person's perspective as being theirs and therefore true for them.
- Identifying similar feelings as part of our own experience.
- Not judging.

When we are empathising with someone else's feelings it is much harder to feel like a victim to them. They stop being a tyrant and become a human being.

An atmosphere of empathy is much more likely to engender trust and a feeling that both parties are prepared to take responsibility for themselves. Honesty can make it easier for people to say what they really want which, in turn, opens up the potential for honest negotiation and a more sophisticated, adult interaction.

Here are some questions that we can ask ourselves to help empathy:

- What does the other person seem to be feeling?
- Have I ever felt a similar thing?
- Have I acted in a similar way to how that person is acting?
- Why did I act in that way?
- Can I forgive myself for acting in that way?
- Bearing in mind that I may be wrong, do I have any idea why the other person might be acting in this way?

You might find it useful to choose three of the questions above and consider your answers.

_____

_____

_____

Step 9: Take back control of the situation

On the basis that the only person we can really change or have power over is ourselves, the key to a less bumpy ride through conflict is to start to take responsibility for our own actions and reactions. When we do this, we spend less time justifying ourselves and more time rectifying our mistakes and moving on from them.

The questions below help us to take back control in a constructive way:

- What, if anything, did you contribute to making this conflict happen?
- With hindsight, what could you have done differently?
- What have you done that has been useful or unhelpful?
- How have you suffered because of your own actions or inactions?
- How have others suffered because of your own actions or inactions?

- What is the most important lesson you can learn from this situation?
- How would it be possible for both perspectives or versions of events to be correct?
- In what way could this conflict improve your work, personal life or your business?
- What is funny or ridiculous about your role in this conflict?
- What would it take for you to let go of this conflict completely?
- What would happen if you did?
- Has your communication been effective in creating an understanding in the other person? What could you have done to improve it?
- What skills could you develop in handling conflict or responding to challenging behaviour?
- Which of the above would it be helpful to take responsibility for or admit to?
- Which of the above are we prepared to forgive ourselves for?

I am not suggesting in any way here that we make ourselves completely vulnerable or are at the mercy of other people who may take advantage of our admittance of guilt. The aim is to take advantage of a bigger picture perspective and see whether the admittance of a failing or oversight on our part may help achieve our wants and needs. It is also to make the most of the opportunity for new thinking, growth or development that the situation will undoubtedly provide.

No one likes making mistakes. Being found out is even worse, but somehow when we admit to ourselves the mistakes we have made we can let them go. Often this helps the other person let them go too and serves as a lesson. This step is only about asking ourselves for forgiveness so that we can move on and get on with the job of pursuing our goals.

Again, it may be useful to choose three of the questions above and answer them as they apply to your situation.

_____

_____

_____

Step 10: Set up the conversation

If we do decide that we need to have a conversation with the other person, the way we set that up may also influence the outcome as will the setting. For example, if we ask someone to have a coffee, we are indicating we want a low-key discussion. The conversation might go something like this:

> YOU: Are you free for a coffee sometime this week?
>
> OTHER PERSON: Why?
>
> YOU: I'd just like to talk through a few things with you. I know we are both busy so I would like to set aside some time to do that.

The other person might ask you to talk about it now or tell you exactly what they want to talk about. That might work for you, in which case you can have the discussion then, or you can suggest that another time would be better as you are too busy.

OR

> YOU: Do you have five or ten minutes to talk about . . .

This is a good way to be clear that you want to talk about a specific issue and set a time limit for that conversation. This can be helpful to focus the conversation or to make sure that it takes place if you or the other person is busy.

A more formal discussion may be in a meeting room with an agenda. There is no doubt that it is easier to set up the conversation in a pre-existing forum, such as performance reviews, but creating new forums and routes for communication can equally adjust the dynamic of the relationship.

You might want to set up the meeting by email. It is helpful to choose the subject of the email carefully to attract the attention of the other person and make it easy for them to accept your invitation to meet. You could entitle this something specific like 'Subject: Performance review'. Alternatively, you might want to use 'Subject: Meeting to discuss way forward' or 'Subject: Can we have a conversation?' or simply 'Subject: Update'.

When heading up your email, think of subject headings that will be attractive to your reader to open and engage with it to avoid procrastination and time delays and to set the tone of the conversation.

In the body of your email, you can continue the invitation and help to make it easier for them to accept it by giving options about timings and framing the meeting as a positive way forward.

So, instead of an email that says:

```
Subject: Meeting to discuss your behaviour

Dear X

We need to meet to talk about the way that you have been
treating me. It is absolutely disgusting.
```

you might have an email that says:

```
Subject: Meeting to discuss way forward

Dear X

I would really like to have a conversation about how we
can work together moving forward. I am available on 2, 4
and 7 September between 9 and 12. When might work for
you?

I imagine we will need no more than half an hour and I
can book a meeting room. If you think we need more time,
let me know.
```

In the second example, it does not hurt us to set up the meeting in a respectful and accommodating way and treat the other person in a way we would want to be treated. This does not mean that we will not want to point out where, for example, we are not happy with the other person's behaviour during the meeting. Rather, we pick our battles and do not unnecessarily create any new ones. We focus on addressing the issues that are important to us and set the tone of behaviour that we are happy with.

There are no guarantees that the other person will engage in the meeting or behave in a way that we would hope or expect. The steps above simply provide an opportunity to make it easier for us and them to start the conversation.

Many of us might wonder why we should need to make such an effort when we think the other person is wrong. The answer is that it is in our best interests to facilitate and clarify the issues and any misunderstandings and give ourselves the best opportunity to get our point across. In other words, by making the act of having the conversation easier for the other person, we give ourselves the opportunity to get what we want and the fact that it also helps the other person does not harm us in any way. On the contrary, it may serve in our favour.

Where we do help the other person to have the conversation in this way, we may be more likely to have an effective one and get closer to meeting our wants and needs. They may also feel more inclined to follow our example in terms of behaviour and even accommodate our wants or needs.

Once we have gone through the previous steps, we will be in a position to do the following:

- Identify what sort of conversation needs to be had, if at all.
- Identify who needs to be involved in that conversation or set of conversations.
- Be clear about what we want to bring to the table.
- Let go of issues which will not help the achievement of our goals.
- Come to the table from a position of physical and emotional strength.
- Succinctly and clearly put forward our case including top and bottom lines.
- Be clear about our desired purpose and outcomes of the conversation.
- Take responsibility for our part in what has happened.
- Take responsibility for next steps.
- Rationally converse with the other person/people.

You might like to do this exercise.

Write down your script or email to the other person or party based on the examples set out above. Do not send it for one day. Then check that it sounds neutral and consider your own response if you were on the receiving end of it.

_____

_____

_____

CHAPTER 7
PRINCIPLE 3: APPLY THE RESOLUTION FRAMEWORK FOR DIFFICULT CONVERSATIONS (STAGE 2)

Stage 2: Having the conversation

Although we can never fully anticipate what will happen in a conversation and how we or the other person will respond, the preparation should have ensured that we have done enough to be able to focus on what is in front of us. Having prepared, we will be less likely to be worrying about information we do not have to hand or to be thinking on the spot about priorities. We will also have done some emotional groundwork.

This chapter provides the tools to build on that work during the conversation and to respond to bumps in the road that may occur during it.

It is helpful to bear in mind that the emphasis on listening and expressing our opinion, wants and needs may vary when we are having a conversation with the person we are in conflict with (and that therefore directly impacts on us) and when we are managing other people in conflict. However, the closer we are able to stick to the tools in both situations, the more likely we are able to bring balance, dignity and professionalism into the presenting situation as well as get our needs met.

Step 11: Practise expansive listening

Listening seems like a basic skill that all of us can do. However, when we are distracted by our own thoughts, feelings and agendas it can become more difficult to listen to other people. Thinking about and practising how we listen effectively can change the tone of the conversation. It can often give us access to more information or clarity about the situation which can open up options.

When we practise expansive listening, we listen with generosity and without judgement and we provide the other person with a space to be heard. Expansive listening is an art not a science. We will need to become increasingly conscious of how we use the skills and adapt them to our style or changing situations. This will take time and for some of us it is an ongoing learning process. During the course of this process, we may read the situation wrongly, lose focus or give the appearance of being judgmental. This may result in the other person withdrawing their trust or displaying emotions that we don't know how to respond to.

In other words, we might make mistakes. In fact, I hope that you make mistakes because they will help you learn the approaches that work for you, your clients and key individuals you interact with and ones that do not. It will also mean that you are being brave in your application of the skills and use of them. Mistakes are useful because they shine a light on our practice, where it is not working or an issue that the other person is having difficulty facing up to or addressing.

The components of expansive listening are:

- empathy
- summarising and paraphrasing
- reframing
- listening behind the words
- holding the listening space
- asking the right questions.

One of the initial challenges for all of us is being willing to listen to other person's challenges in a conflict situation. We immediately might feel that we don't have time, that listening to other people's troubles might bring us down, or that we might simply become irritated or bored with their attitude or what they are saying. We often do not want to admit to this as this trait does not tie in with the fact that we are good, kind and considerate people.

Nevertheless, it is quite a natural reaction, particularly when we think that we have the answer or our opinion is perhaps more valid that the other person's.

As such, again, we need to be honest about our reaction and accept that we are having it. This reminds us that we are not necessarily perfect either and then motivates us to listen with slightly more patience or compassion.

Case study

When working with a group of young people on listening skills, one of them said: 'I don't really want to sit and listen to other people going on about their problems – I have problems of my own.'

She didn't show up to the next class but then came back and continued to voice her discomfort when practising the skills. At the last session, she practised her skills on a group of business people from the local area. These were people with different lives and different experiences but because she had done the course she had developed skills that enabled her to actually help these adults. She summarised the benefit of expansive listening better than I could ever hope to when, at the end of the course she said: 'I realised that listening to other people can make me understand that if I can help other people I can help myself. Through that I have found confidence and am able to speak to people without being aggressive.'

This example illustrates clearly that when we really listen to someone else's challenges it can help to give us clarity on challenges in our own lives and be an equal to that other person whatever our age or social status. Particularly at the beginning, practising expansive listening may feel like it is taking a long time, we can make mistakes and become frustrated. We need to keep in mind that mistakes and frustrations will serve to improve our practice and insight and, in most cases, we will be able to come back from them successfully.

Empathy has already been discussed in the last chapter under Step 8. There is no doubt that it is tricky to practise empathy with someone who we are in conflict with when they are standing in front of us. However, the preparation will help us to start the process of exercising empathy much the same as we might exercise a muscle. The more we practise and exercise, the more natural it becomes to do it. The techniques below should help to keep us in the frame of being empathetic and make it easier to practise empathy as we truly hear the other person.

Summarising and paraphrasing

Summarising and paraphrasing techniques help us to:

- reflect back to the other person what we have heard
- check that we have understood what the other person has said
- let the other person know we are prioritising listening to them.

When we **paraphrase**, we present back to the person what they have been talking about, acting as a verbal mirror. Here is an example:

SPEAKER: I haven't been sleeping and I have been up every night worrying about what my neighbour is going to do next.

LISTENER: So you are having sleepless nights worrying about what your neighbour is going to do next?

SPEAKER: Yes, I am really worried that they are going to do something stupid like tear down the fence.

LISTENER: So you are concerned that they might tear down the fence?

SPEAKER: Yes, or something else. I don't know what they are capable of, they could do anything.

LISTENER: So, you are not really sure what they might do? It could be anything?

At first, it can feel uncomfortable to paraphrase. We can feel as if we are mimicking what the other person has said. This discomfort is generally the only barrier to paraphrasing well. However, when we do it, we often observe a sense of relief coming over the other person that they have had a chance to tell someone what is going on for them and confirm that they have been heard.

Paraphrasing forces the listener to focus solely on the content of what people are telling us and repeating or reflecting back what we have heard. This grounds us in what the other person is actually saying as opposed to what we may be assuming they are saying. It also gives us an opportunity to play back what we are hearing.

In doing this, we are not necessarily agreeing with the other person or telling them that they are right. Rather, that we have fully heard and understood what they are saying. When we do this, the other person will generally either expand on what we have summarised, clarify any misunderstanding they think we may have, or feel they have been heard and move on to what they need to talk about next.

When we **summarise,** we repeat back aspects of what the person has said using fewer words but not changing the nature of what they have said. We pick out key themes and use key words from what the person has said.

When we use summaries, as with paraphrasing we need to be prepared for the fact that we have misunderstood what the other person has said, or may have said, whether by implication or fact. To check that we are correctly reflecting what the other person has said, we may preface our summary by saying something like: 'Correct me if I am wrong but you seem to be saying...' or 'What I am hearing is you think XYZ – have I understood that correctly?' Even when we hear something a certain way, it may not be what the other person is saying, and in order to summarise and paraphrase correctly, we need to be open to the fact that we may have misunderstood the individual.

Equally, when we hear what we say through someone else, it can sound different to the way we normally hear ourselves. So, you may summarise or paraphrase word for word what someone has said and they may come back and say that you have misunderstood them. Initially, we might see this as having made a mistake. However, the speaker may hear what they have said played back to them through you and realise that although this was their initial reaction, on reflection this is not what they want to be saying or indeed thinking. Whether this is because they have not expressed themselves in a way that reflects their true or c or that they

may have onsidered thoughts or you have misunderstood is not important. If we have summarised or paraphrased in a way that does not seem true or resonate with the speaker, we can always recover using the same skills. Here is an example.

> SPEAKER: Anne has a history of being difficult and stopping people getting on with the job. I'm just her next victim.
>
> LISTENER: So you feel that Anne has stopped you getting on with your job?
>
> SPEAKER: No, but I think she will do.

In this case, the recovery will be saying something that shows you have now understood:

> LISTENER: So you think that she will stop you getting on with your job in the future?

What is important is that the listening allows the individual to express themselves, help themselves clarify their thoughts and feel heard. If they challenge what you have said or change it, it means that the reflection has been valuable and served its purpose.

Sometimes it is hard to distinguish what is summarising and what is paraphrasing and there will inevitably be some crossover. The table below gives a picture of the distinction between the two techniques.

Speaker	Listener	
	Summarising	Paraphrasing
My parents have been really ill and it has been a nightmare for me. My father's dementia has got really bad and I don't think my mum is in a state to care for him anymore. She doesn't seem to want to accept that of course so everything is in a state of suspension and it all lands on me. He has had all sorts of accidents around the house and she is not in a fit state to deal with this. To top it all off she has been diagnosed with breast cancer.	There is a lot going on for you as a result of your parents' illness.	Dealing with your father's dementia and your mum's cancer diagnosis has been a nightmare for you. Your mum is having difficulty accepting the situation and you are the only one who can deal with the practicalities of the situation.
I am totally devastated about the whole thing. We are a really close family and I really don't know what I am going to do without them.	This is hitting you hard personally.	You are devastated and thinking about what will happen when they pass away.
I know that I am in a state and probably a bit mad with it all so I thought the Employee Assistance Programme might help as the company is supposed to be saying that they support us and are really mindful of mental health issues but HR hasn't got back to me and the person who was dealing with it now isn't and the other one is leaving.	You want and expect help from the company and you don't feel you are getting it.	This is affecting your mental health and you are not getting the support you expect through the EAP programme. This is exacerbated by the fact that the person who can help you keeps changing role.
It was just about manageable when my husband was around to help for the kids but he has just started a three month contract abroad so he will only be around on the weekends so I don't know what I'm going to do with the kids and work – it's not as if he's going to be earning much more if he goes.	The issue is compounded by the change in your husbnad's work situation and the impact on childcare.	Your husband was able to take care of the kids before but now he has started a three month contract you need childcare and you are concerned about the financial implications of that.
And I'm sorry but I can't believe you haven't seen that I have been struggling. I've phoned in every time I had to deal with an accident at my parents' house and always made up the time or worked from home when the childcare let me down. You even saw me coming out of the bathroom all blotchy faced after I'd heard about my mum.	You think I should have seen the signs that you are upset.	You are really surprised that I haven't seemed to notice your upset for example when you are saying you came out of the bathroom with a blotchy face. You feel you have let me know when you have needed to be with your parents or children. You are often dealing with accidents at your parents' house and you consider that you have made up time lost to deal with your personal responsibilities.
All you seem to want to do is tell me what an awful job I'm doing and tick the boxes so you can get rid of me.	You feel that I am trying to get you out.	You think that I seem to want to just tell you that you are doing an awful job and going through the procedural motions to move you out of your job.

The listener needs to be careful about how they summarise and paraphrase. When people are talking about us or an organisation that we are associated with and are on some level championing or responsible for, the first thing we want to do is respond and put our point of view forward in order to defend ourselves or the organisation. Also, we may try to structure our summaries so that blame does not fall on us and the other person sees our point of view. In these situations, it will be really important to:

- be aware that we will want to defend and justify ourselves
- choose our words carefully so that our paraphrasing and summarising are as neutral as possible
- be prepared to adjust our summaries and paraphrases where they veer towards being argumentative or attempts at self-justification.

When we are a party to the conflict, we should always remind ourselves that we will have an opportunity to respond later, but the first step is to truly practise expansive listening to get the full measure of the other person's perspective.

It is very easy in these situations to infer judgement so we need to find ways to make sure our summaries do not do that. So instead of saying, 'You say I think you are doing a bad job,' you might reflect back with 'You are saying that you think that I think you are doing a bad job.' In this way, we demonstrate a respect for the other person's point of view without may to agree with it. We also avoid creating any perception of judgement which may cause the other person to feel unsafe about setting out their perspective because they are not being heard. This in turn can lead to a shutdown in all or part of the communication which can escalate the conflict again.

<u>Reframing</u>

When we reframe, we effectively summarise or paraphrase in a way that puts a different frame or light on the situation.

> SPEAKER: This has gone on for too long. I don't want to go on like this any longer.
>
> LISTENER: So you really want this to stop and for things to change and be different?

The speaker has not said that they want a change or things to be different, but has said that they don't want things to continue as they are. The listener has inferred from the speaker's somewhat disempowered statement that they want a change and so reframes the more disempowered statement into an empowered one in which the listener might be able to do something about the situation. There is no doubt that the listener's judgement or preferences play a part in the reframing and we need to be careful of forcing rose-tinted glasses on the speaker. Having said this, the speaker will generally let us know if the reframe does not reflect what they are really saying, either by actively disagreeing with what we have said or shutting down and not talking as openly or at all. Again, we can amend our summary, paraphrasing or reframing to reflect the corrections that the speaker has made.

There is a concern that when we listen in this way we might lose what we might need to say to the other person, particularly if we want to explain or justify ourselves. However, if we have prepared in line with Stage 1 in Chapter 6, we can always revert to this and know that we will be able to bring these points up at a later stage. At the same time, listening may mean that we change our initial perspective and are able to move through or let go of some of our original points, concerns or issues and focus on what is most important to us.

When we are listening in this way, we should also avoid questions other than an opener such as 'So tell me what is going on for you' or 'Do you want to talk about what has been happening/causing you concern?' By avoiding questions, we allow people to tell the story and emphasise what is important to them as opposed to what is important to us on the basis of the question we have asked.

Listening behind the words

Listening behind the words means getting underneath what the person is saying. We can do this in a variety of ways:

- Noticing their body language – whether their legs and arms are crossed or they are sweating.
- Listening to important or maybe painful information that they seem to skip over or laugh about when it appears very serious.
- Gently noticing what we feel as they are talking – sometimes the feelings that are triggered in us can reflect their feelings.

We can reflect back the non-verbal communication that we notice as part of our summaries or paraphrasing. When we do this, it is important to acknowledge that it is our experience of what they are saying or how they seem to us.

In this way, we once again leave the door open for the other person to clarify any misunderstandings. For example, 'When you were talking about that situation you rolled your eyes and I am sensing you were frustrated or irritated by what the other person did.'

Hold the listening space

Often the benefits of expansive listening will come through the ability of the listener to be comfortable with silence. This involves waiting for the speaker to find their words and to take the time to formulate their thoughts and get to the bottom of them.

Generally, we only have to wait for a few seconds to give the person a chance to think about what they are saying or add something that they were reluctant to talk about. Again, this can open up the conversation, increase trust and allow for a more honest communication. It can help the other person believe that we are not just listening in order to respond but listening because we are open to hear what is being said.

It can be challenging to control ourselves for those few seconds to allow a bit of space into the conversation, but try it a few times and see how it can change the direction of the conversations in ways we don't always expect.

The more we practise these elements of expansive listening, the more instinctive it becomes and the more successful it can be. The success of expansive listening will be evidenced by a recognition that the person we are listening to feels heard, starts to hear themselves and thinks about and builds upon creative options.

You might like to practise expansive listening. Follow the parameters above and write down how you felt.

_____

_____

_____

What did you sense from the other person in terms of what they felt and thought?

_____

_____

_____

Where did you find ourself judging the other person?

_____

_____

_____

What happened when you allowed for silences?

_____

_____

_____

Step 12: Practise expansive questioning

If we are practising expansive listening, the need for questions reduces as the speaker hears back through the listener what they are saying and answers the obvious questions that have come out of what they have said.

The danger in using questions is that we can use them to direct the speaker's focus towards our assumptions and agendas. So they need to be used with care. Having said that, questions are a great tool for clarifying issues both for the speaker and listener and opening up the options.

The aim of expansive questioning is to facilitate a solution rather than fix a problem. An expansive question will open up the conversation, encourage reflection, elaboration, dialogue and deliberation. Expansive questioning requires us to know that even if we think we know the answer we may not and that the range of answers we may receive are limitless.

Even if we have an impulse to fix, if we can monitor the way we use questions we can translate that impulse into a successful facilitation. All too easily our questions bely our opinions and judgements and can shut down the listener's ability to look to themselves for the solution. So, we need to actively and consciously use open questions to facilitate the speaker.

Generally, we use open questions to open up the conversation and closed questions to drill down on the detail of the response. Simply put, a closed question requests a yes or no answer and an open question does not. But, beyond this, we must remember that the most effective question is one which we do not assume we know the answer to or that does not blame. Instead, we consciously use questions which facilitate the speaker to dig deep and find the whole solution to the problem rather than the limited solution which we as listener can see.

Open questions

The following open questions open up the conversation:

What would you like to talk about?

What do you mean by …?

What would you like me or your colleagues to do about that?

Is there anything else you think we should talk about?

Bear in mind some key questions in coming to a solution are those that you will have already asked of yourself:

What do you want?

What does that look like?

How far are you/we from achieving that?

What do you/we need to do to get you there?

Closed questions

It is also helpful to be mindful of the sometimes less helpful closed questions that can only be answered with a yes, no or one word answer that risk cutting off the conversation:

Do you/I?

Is it/are you?

Can you/I?

Do you want me to go ahead with that?

Checking questions

These are often (but not always) closed in nature but help to continue rapport when summarising and reflecting back. They also give the other person an opportunity to clarify what they mean.

Can I check that ...

How does that sound so far?

Is that your understanding?

Have I got that right?

Expansive questions, also focus on facilitating, as opposed to fixing, in the following way

Fixing questions		Facilitating questions	
What we say	What we can imply	What we say	What we can imply
What happened?	Who was right and who was wrong?	Do you want to talk about what is going on?	Where do you want to start in looking at this situation? i.e. What is important to you in this situation?
Why don't you do []?	Do [] / I know better than you / you can't do it yourself	Have you thought about []....?	I think [] might be worth you thinking about, do you?
Why didn't you do []?	You should do this. You should have done this	If you did [] what might that look like? / If [] then what?	I am suggesting that you think about this. I am not attached to the outcome and I do not judge you for not having thought about it before?
So are you telling me []	I think you are saying [] and it may be difficult to persuade me otherwise	What I am hearing / understanding from you is []. Is that right?	The way I perceive your version of events is [] but I am open to you correcting me/clarifying
Don't you understand []?	I have made a decision about what you do and don't understand	Is it possible to look at this from another angle?	If you changed perspective, could this look different? Are you open to this possibility?

You can practise expansive listening and questioning in the following way:

- Use a very open expansive question to start off the conversation.

- Engage in expansive listening by avoiding questions for at least the first five minutes.

- Before asking the question check what judgements you have — what you think the answer should be.

- Try converting opinions you have like 'Why don't you do this?' into an expansive question like 'Have you thought about doing this?' or 'Do you want to tell me more about your thoughts about this?'

- Check in with yourself by asking yourself if you are leading the person in a certain direction or you are trying to manipulate them to do something.

- Always return to expansive listening in response to the answers to your questions.

- If you get stuck, think about asking the question 'What do you want?' or 'Shall we focus back on what you said you want?'

Step 13: Negotiate

Having prepared for the negotiation, you will have a clear idea of your top and bottom lines and of what is most important to you and what may be important to the other person. You will also have an idea of the key issues and those that you may be more willing to let go of. These need to be clearly front of mind.

We also need to make conscious choices about our strategy and approach. If we are practising all the suggestions, we might find that the nature or the emphasis of the negotiation changes. For example, we may reach agreement on certain issues, additional issues may come up, our fellow negotiator may not react as we expect and our perspective may also change. Accordingly, we need to remain lithe during the course of the negotiation and be aware of our options in terms of negotiation style and strategy as they develop.

Prioritise principles over personalities

The aim in a negotiation is generally to get what you want. Allowing the behaviours of the other person (personalities) to distract us in that process can lose us the opportunity to achieve that.

We can compromise getting what we really want (principles) when we get caught up in our irritation over the other person's behaviour. We lose sight of the principles we are pursuing by getting enmeshed with personality issues. This can cause us to react to the other person rather than pursue our goals and work through the negotiation.

Choose your negotiation strategy

We can tend to adopt a negotiation strategy without considering whether it is the best strategy for the situation. We can also find ourselves responding to the other person's strategy unconsciously and not necessarily in the best interests of the negotiations. So, it is helpful to understand what negotiation strategies we and the other person may consciously or subconsciously be using and continue to evaluate their effectiveness during the course of the negotiation.

Here are some common strategies.

Haggling

When we haggle, we negotiate much as we might when buying or selling on a market stall. One person might start proposing a high figure, the other person will respond with a low figure and they will trade figures until they land on a relatively random point somewhere in the middle that they can, generally reluctantly, agree on.

If you adopt this approach, you need to consider your offers carefully bearing in mind that people are generally prepared to make one big leap from 1 (first offer) to 4 or 5 (1st offer), followed by a maximum of 3 or 4 further negotiated adjustments arriving at say 6 or as our final position. On this basis, if you are negotiating a random trade, ensure that your first offer takes into account the distance the person might need to travel to arrive at a negotiated agreement.

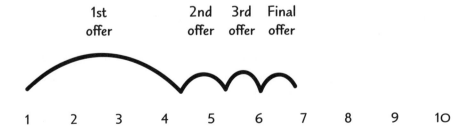

The pros of this strategy:

- It recognises that an agreement can be reached without agreeing that either party is right or wrong.
- It gets the negotiation moving.
- It clarifies the range.
- It recognises the random nature of the risk of continuing the conflict.

And the cons:

- It's difficult to logically justify the agreed result.
- There is a danger of being or feeling out of control.
- There is a danger of alienating your negotiating partner by putting in an unrealistic figure.

'Who blinks first'

'Who blinks first' is the strategy where we try to get the other person to make an offer in the hope that what they offer is slightly better than what we were prepared to agree on. It means that we don't have to expose our hand but it can be a gamble as to who breaks first.

The pros of this strategy:

- It clarifies the other person's expectations.
- It provides a starting point for negotiations.

And the cons:

- You may expose a willingness to settle on better terms than they are willing to offer.
- You may expose a gap between you and your counterpart that requires substantial further negotiation.

Watch my lips

Some negotiators will go in with one figure or position and be clear that they are not prepared to move from this. However, with a little testing, movement is sometimes possible but the approach makes it clear that there is very little room for movement.

The pros of this strategy:

- You are clear on your position and can appear strong.

- Your counterpart may feel that they have to accept your terms for fear that agreement won't be reached otherwise.

And the cons:

- You may appear intransigent to the other people and unwilling to negotiate.

- You may sabotage the opportunity to negotiate within the grey areas.

Seeking the win–win

Through achieving a deep understanding, not just of the other person's negotiating position but the reason why they want what they say they want, allows us to create a possibility for a win–win solution.

In order to do this, we are well served by keeping to the following core principles based on *Getting to Yes* Published by Penguin Random House:

- Focus less on who is right and who is wrong and more on areas of common interests and needs. This means moving away from blame and retribution, which can be hard to let go of. Instead, it involves concentrating on what we both might want and need and, flowing from that, what might work for both of us. It can be summed up simply by the choice 'Do you want to be right or do you want to be happy?'

- Prioritise the generation of creative ideas and options. Key to the generation of these creative ideas and options will be the use of expansive listening and questioning. Also crucially if all parties can commit to this priority, the flow of these ideas and the possibility for play and creative solutions that we have already discussed, open up. However, even if one person allows for expansive listening, the opportunities to generate these ideas and options grow.

- Work together to establish an objective 'norm'. Often the reason we are in a conflict in the first place is that we are applying different standards. It is often difficult for one party to simply agree to the other party's standards. One party might expect the other to start a meeting at 8am, the other party may have worked until 11pm and thinks that 10am is a fair start time. In these circumstances, both parties can look for objective norms: what other people have done, what has happened in similar situations, what experts would say. This may include what other people in the office do or people in other offices do. It may involve speaking to an independent professional or expert or looking at what people have done in the past. The more collaborative the search for these criteria is, the easier they will be to agree instead of them becoming a bone of contention in and of themselves.

These principles are based on Principled Negotiation®, developed at the Harvard Negotiation Project and set out in the book *Getting to Yes* by Roger Fisher and William Ury (plus Bruce Patton for the second edition).

Identify and manage negotiation styles

The Thomas-Kilmann conflict model instrument sets out five overall ways we negotiate. We all have preferred styles that we slip into by way of habit but we can adjust these styles by consciously choosing the best style for the presenting situation. Also, the more familiar we are with negotiating styles, the easier it will be to identify the approach taken by the other party in the negotiation and to work with their style in order to best achieve our goals.

The negotiation style is different from the negotiation strategy. A negotiation strategy includes the practicalities of what we want to achieve and how we are going to achieve it. The Resolution Framework Part 1 set out earlier includes a negotiation strategy which includes looking at top and bottom lines and the process and tactics we will need to achieve them. Part of our strategy will centre around choosing the style of negotiation we wish to adopt to ensure that it is the most effective in the circumstances. When choosing our negotiation style we will balance using a style that is most natural to us with one that is most appropriate for the circumstances. A strategic negotiator will ask themselves:

- Would it be helpful for me to go out of my comfort zone?
- If my negotiation style hasn't been working, is there another alternative?
- Is it better to adopt a style which is most comfortable for me?

Our negotiation style is led by and belies our motivations. These will run on a scale of 'concern for me or us' which triggers a desire to cooperate and, on the other hand, a concern for results which moves us to want to win by asserting ourselves and our needs. According to the Thomas-Kilmann conflict mode instrument, the five key negotiating styles are accommodating, avoiding, competing, compromising and collaborating. (See the website for more details: www.kilmanndiagnostics.com/overview-thomas-kilmann-conflict-mode-instrument-tki.)

Accommodating

This is the approach which leads us to co-operate with the other person without necessarily asserting our own needs. We may do this to display generosity, when we feel we have done something wrong and need to make amends. We may do this when we need to keep the status quo or when we can see that the matters in hand are more important than our own wants and needs. There is a difference between acceding to someone else's needs because we want to and doing it because we feel we have to. In the latter situation, we can feel that we are not getting anything back and develop resentments which are destructive to ourselves and to the relationship. To avoid this scenario, we need to check our motives and take responsibility for our decisions to ensure that we do not fall victim to this decision.

Case study

Freddie was a manager at a small charity and shared many of the projects with Sarah. Sarah had small children and would often come in late or have to leave early or last minute and asked Freddie to cover for her. At first Freddie was happy to help out but he started to feel taken advantage of. He also started to talk about Sarah to colleagues asking them whether they thought the job was too much for her.

Sensing there was a problem, Sarah asked Freddie if there was anything wrong. This gave him an opportunity to say that he felt slightly taken for granted. Sarah realised that she had not shown him the appreciation she felt towards him. They both realised that when Freddie did not feel like covering for Sarah he could say 'Not today'. Sarah also recognised that she needed to do more to help out Freddie when she could.

How can you get the most out of someone who is accommodating?

Asking someone who is accommodating what they need can go far to turn around a situation. Together with this, showing a level of appreciation of any compromises they have made can be particularly effective especially when the accommodating behaviour has created a degree of resentment.

Avoiding

When we are avoiding, we don't co-operate with the other person and we don't assert our needs. It can be helpful to avoid situations that we don't feel able to address or which would be better dealt with by someone else (manager, adviser). However, while nothing is being done about the situation, the situation is unlikely to change and the avoidance can leave people feeling uncertain and unheard.

Case study

Jane was director at a pharmaceutical company. Emma reported to her and they had worked well together for ten years. Emma had been a loyal employee who had outperformed on her targets year on year. When Emma's father fell ill, Emma started to miss targets. Jane felt that her mind wasn't really on the job and that Emma was not performing in client meetings. Jane was concerned that they might lose one of their most important clients who Emma had previously been responsible for. Jane brought in another individual to work with the client and emailed Emma to tell her. Emma asked to set up a meeting to talk about it. Jane said that she would set the meeting up but was too busy at that time. Jane also postponed a few subsequent performance review meetings. Emma kept on trying to speak to Jane and set up meetings with her but the more she tried the more unavailable Jane became.

After many years of loyal service, Emma decided to get a new job. Jane tried to change Emma's mind at this stage but Emma said it was too late.

How can you get the most out of someone who is avoiding?

When someone avoids, we can gently but persistently invite them to engage with us. This is different to sustained and insistent demands. Rather, it lets the person know that it is important to us to engage with them about this but respects their boundaries. Alternatively, or as a fall-back approach where we have tried but failed to engage, we may need to accept that they do not want to address or talk about an issue and work with around that.

Competing

Competing is an assertive but uncooperative approach to a conflict situation. We can adopt a competing approach because we want to stand up for what we believe in or to get the job done. It is also an effective approach in an emergency when people need to act decisively. However, a competitive approach can erode the team or community because it marginalises voices or opinions in attempting to achieve the best result. As a result, even the most well-intentioned competing person may end up being or feeling alienated or misunderstood albeit they achieve the result they had originally intended.

Case study

Jimmy was part of a group of five long leaseholders who all lived in separate flats in a Victorian house. He was also a co-director (along with the other leaseholder) and treasurer of the freehold company which owned the leases on the property. Generally, the other leaseholders had let Jimmy manage the property and make payments as and when they needed to for renovations of the property.

Recently, one of the freeholders, Faisal, had had an accident in his flat which had resulted in carbon monoxide being released into the building. Nobody was injured but there was significant damage caused to the roof.

Jimmy sent Faisal a letter saying that he needed to pay for the full renovation of the property or his lease would be forfeited. He did this without consulting his fellow directors of the freehold company. Faisal's lawyers responded and Faisal confronted a number of the leaseholders. The majority of the leaseholders were very upset at having to be drawn into the situation and confronted Jimmy at a directors' meeting. Jimmy responded by being confrontational and aggresive towards the other freeholders as he felt that he had acted for them in their best interests when they 'couldn't be bothered to do anything themselves'. As a result, the other residents stopped talking to Jimmy and Faisal, factions formed and arguments went on for several months about who was going to pay for the repairs of the property.

How do you get the most out of someone who is competing?

A competitive person can seem like a bulldozer and we can presume that they are hell-bent on getting what they want no matter what. Often, they will be doing this because they think that they have the solution or that they are best placed to deal with a situation.

If we ask someone who is competing what their motives are, we can start to understand why they are taking the action they are taking. This will also allow the competing person to think about what they are doing and demonstrate that they do not necessarily need to tackle the situation alone. Equally, it is helpful to assertively but carefully let the competing person know what our views and commitment to them are.

Compromising

Compromising sits in the middle ground of all the responses. The aim of somebody who is compromising will be to find a solution that will partially satisfy all those involved. The advantage is that some solution is reached and some of the issues, wants or needs are addressed. As a result, it is likely that everyone involved achieves some wins. Compromising can also address issues in a short timeframe without going into too much detail or disruption.

Compromising can be a useful step back from competing and accommodating as we will see. However, compromising will only ever address the surface issues without providing the opportunity to explore the issue in depth.

Case study

Joel was a property investor and Sandy was an interior designer and project manager. They had worked together for many years. Sandy agreed to renovate Joel's property for a fee of £50,000 which Sandy had reduced from £70,000. This was because Joel had promised that he had a very big commercial project coming up that he was going to use Sandy for. The only condition for involvement in the commercial project was that Sandy had to complete Joel's property by June.

During the project, additional work was carried out. Sandy's final bill to Joel was £60,000. Joel asked Sandy for receipts for artisan building work which Sandy did not provide. Joel then said that the works were not finished and required further work which Sandy organised. Joel eventually moved in in September.

As a result of a financial negotiation between their lawyers, Joel agreed to pay Sandy £20,000 but refused to pay the balance because he said that 'Sandy had been sitting on her hands'. He also said that he had proof that she was working on another job while she should have been working on his job. Finally, he alleged that her boyfriend had done most of the work instead of the artisan builder Sandy had promised. Joel suggested that they sit down for a coffee and talk about it. Sandy said that she did not want to discuss it because she couldn't believe that Joel had thought that of her. She just wanted to 'get her money and move on'. That being said, she privately acknowledged that Joel's accusations had some truth to them.

After a set of fractious email exchanges, Joel eventually paid Sandy an additional £35,000 as a final payment. Sandy stopped getting work from people who Joel had previously referred to her and did not get any more work directly from Joel. Eventually, her business which was based on referrals became no longer viable.

Although a compromise agreement was reached, Joel said that he thought that if Sandy had been willing to have a collaborative conversation with him, it is possible that the working relationship may have been salvaged even if she had been guilty of the things that Joel suspected.

How can you get the best out of people who compromise?

It is helpful to identify and acknowledge the compromising person's priorities – speed, avoidance of in-depth discussion – and any other priorities that are also important to you. Once you have done that you can explain that addressing those issues are also a priority for you. If you can simplify them and present them in bite-sized chunks, you may be in a better position to encourage the compromising person to address them.

Collaborating

Collaborating is an assertive and co-operative approach and is at the opposite end of the scale to avoiding a situation. When we collaborate, we enter into in-depth discussions and negotiations to explore the other parties' position, interests and needs as well as clarify our own. The focus of the collaborating parties is on finding a solution that fully meets the needs of those involved.

Collaborating is particularly valuable when a comprehensive solution is required and there are very few, if any, areas which can be compromised upon. It is also particularly useful where those involved need to learn and understand each other or solve a problem through understanding several perspectives. Collaboration can also work to explore the feelings that have been involved in the breakdown of the relationship as well as the facts.

The benefit of collaboration is that the process of exploring the issues in depth and building consensus builds commitment to the solution. In this way, agreements reached are likely to be more sustainable because the parties have worked for and achieved a buy-in to the solution.

Case study

Anthony and Matt had built up a bakery business that had been running successfully for the past 15 years. Anthony had always been very hands-on and Matt had been responsible for the finances. As the business grew, Matt brought in his wife Julie to help run the business. At the time Anthony happily agreed as Julie had been director of finance at a nationwide bakery chain.

Julie and Anthony had a number of small disagreements over the course of the initial months of her tenure. Julie felt that Anthony made irresponsible and ill-thought through purchasing decisions. She also raised concerns about health and safety issues in the bakery and told Anthony that she thought that the day-to-day running of the bakery was shambolic. Anthony said that Julie just wanted to 'splash cash' didn't realise that it was a much smaller operation than the company she previously worked for and she was being dangerously extravagant. When Julie showed Anthony her workings and future plans and projections for the bakery, Anthony said that she was patronising and went to Matt telling him that he wanted to sell his half of the business.

Through a collaborative conversation, Anthony established the following:

- Julie had great experience but his experience was that she was putting him down.
- He didn't understand how the business finances worked so he avoided spending money.
- He knew the bakery needed better financial and operational management.
- He had valuable talents in product and business development.
- He was scared that Julie and Matt were going to try to kick him out of the business.

Julie established the following:

- She had not acknowledged Anthony's previous good work and creative talents.
- She was really keen to get involved in what felt like a great opportunity for her.
- She had been over-zealous about introducing new systems and introducing very corporate systems into a small but growing business.

Matt established the following:

- He wanted a new challenge and to exit the day-to-day running of the business.
- He had not worked through with Anthony or Julie the implications of the changes being put in place.
- He wanted to support the business but he wanted to move into a backseat role.

Following a series of collaborative conversations, Julie and Anthony established their mutual passion for the business and Julie started to demonstrate that she could relieve Anthony of some operational stress. Anthony also felt more heard and appreciated and was able to free up some head space to start to concentrate on new product development and potential strategic opportunities. Once this happened, Julie and Anthony were able to have constructive and creative conversations about the business. From there, they agreed to formally define their roles and consider and agree some concrete plans for future growth including changes in management and structure.

Matt and Anthony realised that although their business relationship had been successful it had changed and it was time for Anthony to be less involved in the business. They acknowledged that they had had an inspirational business relationship which needed to evolve. They agreed that Matt would retain a position as board director while pursuing other interests. They also agreed to have a monthly catch-up breakfast in which they talked about business ideas and what was going on for them so that they could continue to benefit from each other's advice, support and inspiration without necessarily working closely in business together.

Step 14: Follow up

Once the negotiation is completed, we tend to want to walk away from it and expect both sides to follow through on what they have promised. However, we need to allow for the fact that the follow-through may hit bumps in the road. We may revert to old behaviours, we may forget to follow through or we may simply be unable to deliver on our promises.

This can create a new set of resentments and conflicts very easily, particularly due to the added expectation that the matter was to be resolved. So, it is helpful to plan for these bumps in the road with agreed follow-ups with respect to certain actions and to anticipate how the parties may work together and communicate to resolve the situation should things not go according to plan in the future.

In cases where a transaction is easily completed following a negotiation, the follow-up can be very straightforward and may extend to an email confirming that something has happened – money has been paid for example. However, if the negotiation has involved an ongoing relationship, it may be helpful to plan times for follow-ups, establish what will be covered and when and prepare in a similar way to the initial negotiation.

Equally, if the result of the negotiation is for actions to be taken that are dependent on other people, an agreed set of dates for follow-up or notifications of key actions can avoid the need to re-engage in the conflict. For example, in the case of an agreement between neighbours about the removal of a dead tree, an agreed follow-up plan may include:

● notification that the local council has been contacted (within a certain period)

● confirmation that the council had received the request and details of their timetable

● notification of approval by the council

● notice of the date of removal of the tree

● a date for follow-up in case of delay more than six months from the date of the negotiation.

CHAPTER 8
PRINCIPLE 4: MANAGE THE RESOLUTION – THE SOFT MEDIATION ASSIGNMENT

This chapter will take you through the process of supporting two parties to resolve a relatively low-level conflict by adopting the role of 'resolution agent'. As well as suggesting tools to practise, it will give you principles to work to. It is very unlikely that you will work to all the stages of the 'assignment' at once. Take your time and be prepared to ask for help. Broadly, we will cover the following stages of resolving low-level disputes as follows:

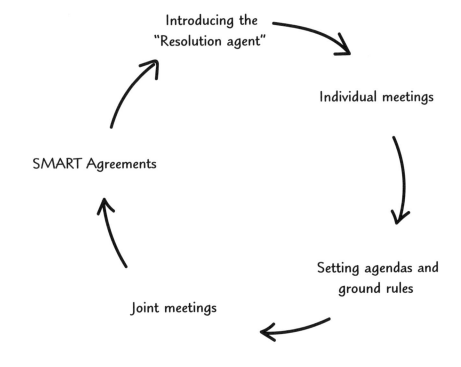

The role of the resolution agent

Often, parties involved in a dispute refer to a third party for assistance in finding a conclusion to it. This may be someone with some actual or perceived authority such as a manager or a housing officer, or it could be an HR officer. In each of these cases that third party will have some sort of interest in the issue or have some sort of authority over the parties. As such, they won't be a mediator or formally mediate as they will not have the impartiality of the mediator. However, notwithstanding their personal interest, if they practise the following steps they will have a good chance of enabling the parties to find a solution in a similar way to a mediator, without having to escalate the situation.

The term 'resolution agent' is used here although different organisations and individuals may use a different name or not give them a defined name at all. The resolution agent will perform many of the same tasks and roles as the conflict coach and the mediator and the role of the conflict coach may develop into that of resolution agent. The difference will be that generally the resolution agent will have an investment in the parties achieving a resolution.

This is slightly different to the role of a conflict coach or mediator who should not have an agenda other than that defined by the parties. This may include, but may not be limited to, resolving the situation with the other person. The process will be coloured by the resolution agent's interest and the fact that they are in a way a party in the conflict. However, it will also represent the reality of the situation – what the company, housing association or manager wants or expects – and ground any conversations in that reality.

As with the conflict coach, the role of the resolution agent can be a tricky one and will require some training, practice and support. This is useful to bear in mind when using some of the tools set out below, to the degree that where you are finding the role challenging or the principles tricky to apply, you can always pause the process, take time to consider and get help.

In order to keep clear boundaries around the resolution agent's role and therefore create a feeling of safety in the process, transparency is very helpful and the resolution agent will need to work to the following principles to keep the process a safe one and to ensure all cards are on the table.

Introducing yourself

The resolution agent will need to create an environment in which both parties feel they can be open and honest with them. To achieve this, the resolution agent will need to:

- candidly state their interest in the issue and their desire for the matter to be resolved (if indeed they do want a resolution)
- avoid arguing for or against their desired outcome during the course of discussions
- explain their commitment to being as impartial as possible in the circumstances
- avoid providing solutions
- suspend their own judgement
- work and support the parties
- demonstrate their faith in the parties' abilities to resolve the issue by not providing solutions
- keep confidential any information that each of the parties have given them
- be willing to refer to a mediator or someone else if they feel out of their depth.

A good way of demonstrating these qualities from the get-go is by putting together an opening script to start the process of introducing your intention to help the parties to resolve the situation and the role you plan to play. If you prepare this script and say the same thing to both of the parties separately or together, it will go far to demonstrate your commitment to being impartial and the principles you are adhering to. This may go along the following lines:

'I want to help you to resolve this because [it is affecting you as individuals but it is also affecting the team]. I believe that you can find a solution that will work for you and that helps you to get to the other side of this situation whatever that looks like. I am going to keep confidential anything you say to me individually and I won't judge you in this process. If you tell me something that I think will be helpful to tell . . ., then I will let you know and you can think about whether or how you want to tell them or want me to tell them. Also, if I hear anything that I think might be helpful to feed back to the company, I will tell you what that is and we can discuss whether or how you wish to deliver that feedback. I also won't be telling you what to do, but instead I hope to help you find your own solutions which I trust you can and will.'

To practise this skill, in your own words write down your introduction in supporting others to resolve their conflict.

_____

_____

_____

Structuring the resolution process

Although it is important to allow a degree of flexibility in the resolution process, taking account of the fact that people may have specific preferences and things may change, it is also helpful to start with a plan of how the process might work. Essentially, this will work through a series of individual and joint meetings and in some cases by the resolution agent passing information from one party to another.

It is helpful to set out the options that you might follow to the parties so that they will be aware of what you are doing when you are doing it. You might also want to say at the beginning that you may need to spend more time with one party than the other and this will not be because you are on one party's side more than the other but rather to explore the issues in an effort to support both.

Holding individual meetings

First, set up times to have individual meetings with each of the parties before bringing them together. This is crucial for the following reasons:

- It develops a relationship of trust and confidence with each of the parties.
- It helps them identify key issues and priorities.
- It helps them work out what they want to say to the other person.
- It evaluates whether there is room for the parties to talk.

- It identifies potential common ground.
- It identifies potential areas of non-agreement.
- It establishes whether the resolution agent is the best person to help the parties.

Actual and perceived fairness will be crucial to the success of these initial meetings and of gaining the confidence of the parties. This will be easier to achieve if the meetings are of a similar length and the same approach is taken (expansive listening and questioning, clarification and prioritisation of issues) and during the process, the resolution agent does not appear to show a preference to one party over the other.

The success of this part of the process is crucial because perceived unfairness will generally cause the person who sees themselves as not being favoured to react adversely.

Case study

Jack and Josie had been at loggerheads for several months. They were vying for the director position. Jack had said that Josie and the company were discriminating against him due to his time off sick and Josie said that Jack's performance was below par and that he was letting down the team. Abid, their vice president, set himself out as the resolution agent. However, he gave Josie the lion's share of work in conducting their day-to-day business and so spent more time in meetings with her and building a relationship with her.

Abid started to notice that Jack's protests made him feel less supportive of Jack. In the circumstances, Abid decided to refer the issue to an independent mediator to ensure that the matter was dealt with carefully. In doing so, he felt more confident that issues of process and partiality would not interfere with the resolution or escalation of the issue.

Of course, if Abid had been able to talk this through with Jack then it may have worked, but because of the actual and perceived partiality, this would have required a fairly sophisticated skillset on Abid's part that he was happy to accept he did not have. As a result, the matter was resolved to the satisfaction of all the parties and Abid's relationship with Jack was also given the room to settle down and rebuild.

Keeping confidentiality will in some circumstances be challenging. It is far more realistic to accept that certain issues may be difficult to keep confidential such as matters that come to light that may damage the organisation or people in it. While most of the time it should be possible to have off-the-record conversations, it is preferable to discuss before the conversations what happens if information comes to light that the resolution agent feels may need to be shared. To help create clarity, the resolution agent might say:

> 'I want to make sure that this is a safe space for you because being able to have open conversations is likely to significantly help us resolve this issue. I am happy to have off-the-record discussions, but you need to know that if you tell me anything that makes me concerned of a risk to the organisation or its stakeholders or clients, then we might have to talk about how I can best deal with that information. You also need to know that I may be under a duty to disclose that information.'

It is preferable for the resolution agent not to communicate anything on behalf of either of the parties. However, if you are in a situation where that is absolutely necessary, make sure you:

- write down anything either of the parties want to communicate to the other party or the organisation
- check that what they have written down is what they want to say
- double-check that they want to communicate it
- check if there is anything else.

Holding joint meetings

Much can be achieved through joint meetings which they can often lead to the parties coming together to have a conversation with each other that is reasonable and does not have to be facilitated.

The resolution agent's main role in a joint meeting will be to create the environment conducive to reaching an outcome to the situation that they can live with.

Managing the agenda

This will include ensuring the parties have a clear agenda and supporting the parties to keep to the agenda and designated timings.

Establishing ground rules and boundaries

Ground rules and boundaries are there to support the resolution agent as much as the parties and may include the following:

- Everyone having time to speak without being interrupted.
- Everyone keeping to time.
- No abusive language or behaviour.
- A commitment to keep the content of meeting discussed confidential or to agree what will be disclosed at the end of the meeting to whom and by whom.
- Roles the resolution agent will or will not play.

Create the space for the parties to hear themselves and each other

One of the most effective roles of the resolution agent is being present while the parties develop a conversation between themselves. To create this space, the resolution agent will use expansive listening and questioning which should effectively not only mirror what the speaker is saying but also help the listener hear the speaker's point of view from another person's point of view.

Focus the resolution

Part of the expansive listening and questioning used by the resolution agent will have the effect of supporting the process of defining next steps, areas of agreement and follow-up. By punctuating the conversations in this way, the resolution agent will help the parties build a set of actions or plans that can support the parties to find a way forward culminating in a SMART agreement (discussed below).

<u>WARNING: Know your limits</u>

Above all, acting as a resolution agent requires practice of the principles. You need to watch out for questions or even body language (the raising of an eyebrow) that may bely your prejudices and alienate the parties from trusting you. The key will be applying the principles to the degree that you feel comfortable and extricating yourself when you don't.

It may be that rather than going ahead with a joint meeting, for example, you stick with separate meetings and practise the principles in this way. This will ensure that you have helped the parties fully clarify their positions, interests and needs as well as their individual strategies for a way forward.

Following a joint meeting or set of separate meetings to ground the issues, you may then want to carry out a joint meeting as you may usually do in your normal role. If you do this, you might want to say 'I am taking my resolution agent hat off now and putting my manager hat on. Is that OK?'

Equally, if you start to feel out of your depth in a joint meeting, if the conversation seems to deteriorate and does not follow a flow or keep to the agenda, don't be afraid to pause or suspend the process and get some help. The golden rule here is: IF IN DOUBT, DON'T. In other words, if you don't feel comfortable or in integrity, in other words, you feel like you are compromising your standards or beliefs during the course of trying to support people through a conflict situation, don't. Even though it may not feel like it, there is generally time to get the right person in and remedy the situation.

Enabling SMART agreements

The most effective agreements are generally those that have been carefully constructed rather than imposed. The principles of SMART agreements provide the infrastructure to construct those agreements. Key to this process is the understanding that the resolution agent and the parties should not expect to resolve all the issues at once. Instead, they

● should clarify areas for agreement and non-agreement, work on each area of agreement and build the terms of agreement around that area, and then agree what to do about the areas of non-agreement.

SMART agreements are generally more sustainable because they create buy-in and clarity. They are Specific, Measurable, Agreed, Realistic and Time-bound and this is achieved in the following way.

Specific

Being specific is being clear about who is going to do what, to whom and when. If an agreement is not clearly understandable, then it is probably not specific enough. When building these agreements, it is important to be prepared to ask for clarification when we don't understand in order to avoid confusion later down the line. Useful questions to ensure that agreements are specific can include:

What exactly do you mean by that?

Who will do what to whom?

Can you list all the things you want to achieve through that action?

Often, when we reach broad agreement, we become reluctant to drill down into the detail for fear of rocking the boat and creating disagreement again. When we feel like this it is a reminder that we should not expect conflict resolution to be a straight line. It is normal to come in and out of being in agreement when we drill down into the detail. It is in fact this process of looking at the points of detail that will be instrumental in helping the parties to fully resolve, and crucially let go of, past issues as well as create options for the future.

Measurable

Ensuring an agreement is measurable means being able to clearly demonstrate the fact that the actions agreed have been completed or the level to which they have been fulfilled. Useful questions to help create measurable actions include:

How will you know when this has happened/been achieved?'

What will success look like?

What steps will need to be achieved for that to happen?

Agreed upon

It is not enough for everyone to say yes and go through the motions when an agreement is reached. Buy-in is key to the sustainability and workability of any agreement. Buy-in means that people feel like they have had a part in forming and creating the agreement. The consequence of this will be that they are invested in making it work and, crucially, they feel that they can follow it through. Without buy-in people can feel that the agreement does not reflect their opinions or was reached despite them. In these cases new resentments can build upon the existing conflicts and fundamental sustainable agreements are not reached.

So, somewhat counter-intuitively, to ensure a true agreement with buy-in, it is helpful to test the agreement using questions such as:

How likely is this option to work?

Are you comfortable with this?

I can see that you are a bit hesitant, so is there anything you want to talk through before committing to this?

After each point has been agreed, the parties should have a chance to read, consider and confirm their agreement. Obviously, this should not be laboured as time, financial and other considerations may reasonably create pressure for an agreement to be reached. But a balance needs to be achieved to ensure parties really are going to do what they say.

Realistic

This may seem obvious but we need to be mindful of not setting the agreement up to fail by being unrealistic. The other elements of the SMART agreement will help to ground the provisions in reality, particularly the specific, measurable and time-bound elements. While it is good to set ambitious goals and work towards achieving them through the agreement, it is also helpful to keep asking how realistic it is, not to undermine the agreement but rather to test it and to ensure that it can work.

Time-bound

This is the 'by when' element of the agreement. A SMART agreement will often be broken down into stages and it is helpful to put timings to every stage. Often these will be deadlines that will not be moveable, but sometimes there may be flexibility. It is also possible that timings may need to change for whatever reason and so conversations will need to be had and agreements reached about what will happen if timings slip knowing that while this will not be the plan, it might happen.

CHAPTER 9
PRINCIPLE 5: BUILD A CULTURE OF EARLY CONFLICT RESOLUTION

This chapter is intended to support you build a culture of early resolution. This means creating an environment in which individuals are enabled to take responsibility for the conflict situations they find themselves in and learn and grow from them. The intended end result goes beyond a reduction of court battles and the emotional stress and financial consequences that result, replacing them with a more functional, empowered, efficient working environment.

Through a good culture of conflict resolution, we become much more efficient and creative. We place ourselves in a position to create and build unity despite, and sometimes because of, our differences.

We will focus mainly on workplace infrastructures as they are rich with relationships and interactions that replicate other organisations, associations and communities. We will also look at how similar principles can be introduced into schools and communities to build sustainable early resolution cultures and change.

This principle sets out a comprehensive approach to building a culture of early conflict resolution. However, most of the component elements that make up that culture can be used as standalone strategies or interventions that can be built upon piece by piece.

Early resolution in the workplace

Introducing a culture of early resolution into the workplace is effectively a change process. What this will mean in practice is the introduction of new ways of thinking in terms of policies, procedures and, crucially, habits. These will supplement as well as complement processes, such as the grievance and disciplinary processes or investigations, which are set up to help us assign responsibility, without doing away with them altogether.

New early resolution mechanisms will allow for situations which may be slightly grey. Although it will continue to be important to retain systems to 'right wrongs', a culture of early resolution will mean that grievance, disciplinary and investigatory processes may cease to be the go-to solution. Rather, the solution will be one which does not further divide the parties while still addressing their needs and concerns. Because of the cultural change which sits alongside the need to preserve all routes to pursue human and other rights, a staged approach is required.

The stages may be interchangeable and need some flexibility depending on the existing culture and practice of the organisation.

Step 1: See whether or how mediation works

In the past, I used to be cautious about introducing mediation into an organisation without any training or reference to it in employee handbooks. This was because if mediation was suggested out of the blue to individuals there was a risk that those individuals would feel alienated or become defensive. This alienation would derive from the fact that individuals did not quite understand the process and felt threatened by it – 'Why me?' or in other words 'Why have I been singled out to do this when nobody else has?'

The result reported to me by HR professionals who wanted to refer a matter to mediation was often that when it was proposed, the parties chose not to enter the process and continued with the disciplinary and grievance process (which often did not end well for either party). Although this can still be the case, the increased use of mediation has normalised it to some degree and it is not unusual for those in dispute to even request mediation themselves. It is much more widely accepted that mediation is increasingly used and accepted as a viable option or solution, whether or not policies provide for it.

Having said that, organisations and individuals will not want to jump into mediation blind. So, the best way to test the process is to introduce in the first instance a seasoned mediator, or set of mediators, to conclude a few cases and compile feedback from those cases.

The introduction of a trained mediator who will remain true to the process at this stage is really important in order to fully evaluate whether and how it can work. Offering mediation can be a light touch process where HR or the manager says something along these lines:

> 'I would like to offer you the opportunity for you to mediate with . . . . If you want, you can have a confidential discussion with the mediator to find out more about how it works and if it is something you want to do. You can then get back to me and let me know.'

To evaluate the benefit, there could be feedback to the mediation commissioner by the parties immediately following the mediation, and after a period of say three to six months after that.

Feedback will relate to the process not to the detail of the dispute and should include:

- How useful did you find the mediation process?
- Without referring to the detail of what happened, what did you find useful and what did you find unhelpful?
- As a result of this process, is there any general feedback you would like to give back to the organisation?
- If you were in a similar situation again, would you choose to mediate?

Step 2: Establish the business case for mediation and early resolution

This section looks at gathering and analysing the information required to make decisions about whether and how to take a new approach to conflict resolution.

The conflict audit

A conflict audit is a light touch but effective audit of the success (or otherwise) of the following:

- an organisation's current formal and informal processes and practices when addressing conflicts at an early stage
- the effectiveness of its management of the escalation of conflict
- the impact of those practices on the organisation, its people and its clients or customers.

The audit comprises four questionnaires which are broadly similar in content but taken from the perspective of different individuals and functions within the organisation.

Employee questionnaire

The employee questionnaire (see Appendix 1) should be given to as many employees as possible to give the fullest picture of employees throughout the organisation. It gets a picture of how the employee views the organisation and their options in the event of challenge and encourages the employee to be honest as opposed to critical.

It should be completed in addition to the other function questionnaires where, for example, the employee is a team lead, but not in conjunction with the stakeholder questionnaire.

Director/team lead questionnaire

The director/team lead questionnaire (see Appendix 2) is a very short questionnaire that gives a top-line view of management trends. It looks at the tangible cost of conflict in terms of time spent by higher paid members of the organisation. The director/team leader is also best placed to identify direct financial losses or potential losses arising from the conflict which again give an indication of the appropriate remedies and level of investment required.

Head of legal/HR/finance questionnaire

The head of legal/HR/finance questionnaire (see Appendix 3) is best completed by each of the legal, HR and finance departments to provide the fullest picture possible. Of course, sections can be lifted depending on the department but with the three departments working together, we can achieve the most comprehensive analysis of the facts as they are presenting themselves within the organisation.

Client/stakeholder questionnaire

The audience for the client/stakeholder questionnaire (see Appendix 4) will range from clients to stakeholders and funders and will focus on the relationship they have with the organisation and the individuals that comprise it. This section of the questionnaire borders on being a customer satisfaction survey. However, it goes beyond customer satisfaction to understand:

- what the client or stakeholder thinks of the relationship with the organisation or its people
- indications of actual or possible loss of opportunity.

It is important that this survey is short and easy to complete. In putting the survey to clients and stakeholders, the organisation has an opportunity to communicate that it values these relationships and seeks to improve the quality of these working relationships.

Each of the questionnaires are worded to obtain the most honest and unbiased response from the person answering. For this reason, they may include questions that seem obvious to HR or management such as 'Does the organisation have an informal process to deal with conflicts and agreements?', but will gain a better perspective of what the employee or client knows about that process and how they engage with it.

Analysing the audit

The audit will provide a picture of facts and perceptions. What you do with the information flowing from it will depend on the priorities of the organisation. What the audit should provide is information to assess how conflict affects the following areas of the business:

- employee engagement
- leadership
- process management
- brand
- finance
- future business and funding relationships.

Engagement

Good conflict management will often go hand in hand with high levels of employee engagement. By that, I mean engendering healthy relationships within the organisation. This includes good mutual communication which leads to employees feeling appreciated and appreciative.

Key to engagement is members of the organisation feeling that they are motivated in their work. An engaged employee will feel that working in the organisation is aligned with their own goals. They might also feel that that if they do a good job it will be of benefit to both the organisation and themselves. In other words, the relationship between the organisation and the individual is interdependent and each party contributes something of value.

In conflict situations, individuals are less likely to be engaged with the organisation and the people in it. We can feel that the behaviour of certain individuals represents the attitudes of the organisation as a whole and so disengage from the organisation and its values. However, in situations where we are enabled by the organisation to overcome these conflicts and feedback and learn through them, our self-esteem and respect for the organisation can turn around and provide an opportunity to increase engagement.

Research shows higher stress is associated with lower work satisfaction, lower levels of loyalty to line management and a higher intention to leave the organisation David Guest: *Human Resources Management Journal* 2004. Research (by CIPD in https://www.cipd.co.uk/Images/getting-under-skin-workplace-conflict_2015-tracing-experiences-employees_tcm18-10800.pdf) also shows that stress is the second biggest cause of workplace conflict after personality clashes and employees spend a day a month dealing with this on average. Evidence further demonstrates that improving employee engagement correlates with improving performance and profitability (details of this are set out in the MacLeod Review http://dera.ioe.ac.uk/1810/1/file52215.pdf).

Sickness and leave will be a big indicator of the effect of conflict on engagement or otherwise, particularly in cases where people find it difficult to work through conflict situations for whatever reason.

Engagement, or the lack of it, can be as much about what people are thinking about doing as what they are doing. For example, if they are considering raising a grievance or taking sickness leave as alternative options, it is an indication that they are distancing themselves from the organisation. If they do not take the sickness leave or raise the grievance, it is likely that they will hold a resentment that might be stronger than the original upset and may mushroom. What I often hear people say is that 'I didn't go on sickness leave or bring a grievance [out of loyalty][because I had committed to get the job done][because I didn't want to create a problem] and now they are doing [] to me.

Case study

Rory felt continually bullied by his boss. He was continually told that he should be working additional hours even though this was outside his remit. Rory had heard other employees talk about similar experiences with the same individual. He worked the additional hours but began to feel very depressed and developed severe eczema.

Rory went to his doctor who suggested he take a week off to allow himself the opportunity to recover. He did not take the time out of loyalty to the organisation. When the situation did not change, he felt even more upset that he had sacrificed his help and not taken an opportunity to recover. This increased his resentment towards his boss and the organisation. He started to talk to his colleagues about it and the team became very disillusioned with the organisation's treatment of its employees.

With this in mind, key sections of the audit that are likely to highlight employee engagement or otherwise include the following:

- Employee questionnaire: Questions 4 to 10, 12, 13 and 16.
- Director/team lead questionnaire: Question 1.
- Head of legal/HR/finance questionnaire: Questions 1 to 5, 7, 10 and 11.

Leadership

In an organisation where there is effective leadership, early resolution is an integral part of the culture. This means that leaders are able to be comfortable with conflict. This is not to say that they enjoy it or create it but rather they understand and accept that it will arise and are confident in their ability to work through it. Crucially, leaders are equipped to manage their own conflict and conflicts within their team and do not feel the need to bring in HR whenever they have a problem or issue with an employee.

Working with HR and other parts of the organisation will be important, but critically the effective leader will not hand over all responsibility for managing the issue when HR starts to become involved. The parts of the audit that build up the picture of leadership within conflict situations are the following:

- Employee questionnaire: Questions 4, 7, 10 to 12, 14 and 16.
- Director/team lead questionnaire: Questions 7 to 9.

Process management

The process analysis relates not only to the processes themselves but how they are being used and responded to. How much is too much grievance, disciplinary action and sick leave will depend on the organisation and its values.

I put the long-term sick in the same category as grievances and disciplinary action because organisations we have worked with have found that many proposed grievance actions have been averted by an employee going off sick due to the stress caused by the conflict. Indeed, the support and management of mental and physical health is a crucial component of these processes if they are to be effective and sustainable. For example, the stigma of being in a grievance or disciplinary process, or being the accused victim or perpetrator of discrimination, can be associated with a diagnosis of depression (https://www.nice.org.uk/guidance/cg90).

In evaluating and making decisions in this area, you will also need to be honest about your organisation's priorities. It may be that you want to send strong messages about certain types of behaviour or shut down challenges. This may be the case where a number of claims have been brought and the organisation wants to send a message to discourage people from bringing such claims. Such a strategy is risky in terms of engagement, brand image and financial risk and is discouraged in the Principles. Having said that, as with most things, the more clarity and information the organisation has about what works and what doesn't, the more effective it will be for all within the organisation.

The analysis will clarify how the processes are working and used and how employees experience them. This in turn will enable the organisation to be better equipped to foresee not only the benefits but also the consequences of current systems. The following questions support that process:

- Employee questionnaire: Questions 1 to 4, 15 and 16.
- Director/team lead questionnaire: Questions 7 to 9.
- Head of legal/HR/finance questionnaire: Questions 1 to 5, 8 to 12.

Brand

The way an organisation manages conflict will have an immediate impact on its brand. Organisations are rated on what they are like to work for when attracting talent. In addition, the use of social media makes the risk of a company being discredited, even temporarily, by unhappy employees very real.

Workforces are becoming increasingly emotionally intelligent. As the use of coaching, mentoring and mediation grows, there is an increasing openness and indeed expectation to receive access to these resources. The workforce and clients also have higher expectations than may have previously existed about the capacity of senior executives to manage complex relationship issues.

However, many organisations have struggled to keep up with these expectations for a plethora of very good reasons, most notably competing resources or a feeling that this is already dealt with. The absence of a sophisticated strategic organisational response to conflict resolution beyond the standard grievance and disciplinary processes can have a number of damaging repercussions.

More people than would care to admit walk along the street to work planning and plotting what they are going to say to someone they are bumping up against at work. The more the scenario goes around in our heads, the more entrenched we can become and most of the time this process polarises our position and can set us at loggerheads both with the individual and the organisation as a persona in its own right.

Case study

Anastasia was an advertising professional struggling to manage Ellie, one of her team members. Anastasia believed that Ellie was not performing her own functions and was trying to muscle in on Anastasia's job. In particular, Anastasia felt that the brief instructions were not followed and many members of departments working closely with Ellie complained regularly about her attitude and her ability to get the job done.

Anastasia had been working from home during certain periods due to an ongoing medical condition. When Anastasia was out of the office, Ellie responded to group emails without Anastasia's authorisation as she thought that it was important to get the job done. This left Anastasia feeling threatened and defensive as she found that Ellie was continually undermining her.

Anastasia kept pulling Ellie up on her performance and on this undermining behaviour. Ellie then went to the director who Anastasia reported into and told him that she felt bullied by her. Anastasia went to see the same director and told him that Ellie was performing poorly and undermining her. Anastasia said that she thought that the issue might be one of communication and asked for some coaching support or, if necessary, mediation.

The director said that he was not prepared to discuss the situation at all and referred the matter to the HR department. Various requests were made by Anastasia to HR for a formal mediation that were ignored and eventually refused. At the same time, Ellie issued a grievance against Anastasia for bullying and Anastasia's medical condition worsened to the degree that she went off sick for two weeks on the strict instruction of her doctor.

Anastasia asked again to receive some training or coaching to help her deal with the situation or for a mediator to come in. She felt that it was important that someone appropriately qualified to create the circumstances favourable to having a constructive conversation intervene, and did not feel that this was something that the HR department could provide as she couldn't shake the feeling that they were acting for the company and had an agenda.

The request to mediate was refused and Anastasia was told that coaching was only available for directors. Anastasia felt angry and upset with the organisation about this saying: 'I spend a lot of time at work, I want to know that when things go wrong in my relationships with other people there needs to be a solution that doesn't put me at odds with the people I work with every day. I want to say to the organisation "What is your excuse for not having mediation as a process we can revert to."'

Having worked with a number of other people in similar situations, the sentiment has been similar. This is what people have said to us when mediation has been refused by their organisation:

'Businesses have a personality, when you work for a business, you have a relationship with it. My employer held itself out as cutting edge and up to date but refused to mediate. For me that was a significant mixed message and resulted in me losing faith in and being excited about the brand.' (Head of department of London-based division of a global brand)

'Not dealing with underlying issues at play within teams affects the invisibles: brand reputation, brand perception, brand integrity get tarnished . . . it doesn't have to be that way, it could be another way.' (Marketing Director of UK fashion house)

Case study

Anastasia spoke to her informal mentor, a director within the organisation, who said that was how the organisation treated people and why she was leaving. The mentor had been engaged by the organisation as such and hence the informality of the arrangement. They also had not told anyone in the organisation about her own concerns as there was no point feeding this back.

How employees and customers feel that they have been treated by individuals within the organisation will have an impact on the way they view the organisation and the way they talk about the organisation. Slowly and subtly, but necessarily, this has an impact on the organisation's brand. Key sections of the audit that highlight how your conflict affects your brand include:

- Employee questionnaire: Questions 5 to 8, 10 to 16.
- Director/team lead questionnaire: Questions 3 to 6.
- Head of legal/HR/finance questionnaire: Questions 1, 3 to 5, 7, 10 to 11, 13 to 14.
- Client/stakeholder questionnaire: Questions 2 to 6.

Finance

The decision whether to introduce mediation or early conflict resolution can, in the first instance, be based on what the business or team is losing out on if it does not resolve conflict earlier.

It can be challenging to identify the need to invest in early resolution processes because of the challenge arising in how and when conflict may occur and other pressing priorities of the business.

Even without an audit, employers are well advised to be aware of the potential financial as well as social cost of conflict in the context of the mental health of its workers.

The standard escalation of conflicts through to grievance and disciplinary action is a costly, time-consuming and stressful process. In a purely financial audit of a standard case that had gone to tribunal carried out on one of our clients, we discovered they had incurred the following costs as a minimum:

Cash cost of compromise agreement	£30,000
Legal cost of grievance, investigation and tribunal	£30,000
Internal management time (20 days)	£24,000
60 sick days	£15,600
Opportunity cost	£20,000
Total cost	£119,000

Claims to be brought by employees constitute an increasing risk in the UK. In 2013 tribunal fees were introduced and the number of claims reduced by 70%. This effect is likely to be reversed in view of the 2017 UK judgement ruling that employees should not have to pay a fee to bring a claim to tribunal and the commitment (at the time of writing) of the UK government to stop charging fees and refunding those who paid fees for employment tribunal claims and appeals.

In many cases, the anxiety and stress of conflicts at work are the trigger or reason for exacerbation of existing mental-health issues. In the UK one in six people in the workplace experience mental distress, depression or stress-related problems at any one time. In 2007, economic inactivity among 72% of men and 68% of women was as a result of mental health problems (see the report 'Pay the price': www.kingsfund.org.uk/publications/paying-price).

The Organisation for Economic Cooperation and Development estimates that mental ill-health costs the UK around 4.5% of GDP in lost working days, reduced productivity and higher benefits spending. Specifically, it has been reported that 140 million working days are lost to sickness absence. It was also found that employers pay £9 billion a year in sick pay and associated costs, plus the indirect costs of managing business while people are off sick (see the 2011 government report: Health at Work: An independent review of sickness absence https://www.gov.uk/government/publications/review-of-the-sickness-absence-system-in-great-britain).

I should be very clear that the workplace conflict is not the only cause of mental-health issues at work. Nor are the principles a cure all for the financial consequences of mental-health issues in the workplace. However, the audit can highlight where areas of risk for the organisation and its employees may lie.

The cost–risk analysis set out above identifies the main heads of evaluating the cost of conflict:

- cash cost of compromise agreement
- legal cost of grievance, investigation and tribunal
- internal management time
- sick days
- opportunity cost.

The audit will also help to analyse and specify these costs as they apply to the organisation in the following sections:

- Employee questionnaire: Question 12.
- Director/team lead questionnaire: Questions 1 to 6 and 9.
- Head of legal/HR/finance questionnaire: Questions 6 to 14.
- Client/stakeholder questionnaire: Questions 4 to 6.

Future business and funding relationships

Very simply, when employees are not motivated to be helpful or even civil with their customers, that may cause the customer or client to not come back or to feel uncomfortable about engaging with the organisation. Being in the mindset of providing a service can be challenging when we are worrying about ourselves, our futures and our feelings and that will quickly have an impact on relationships with clients and key relationships.

Case study

Jeremy worked in a successful advertising team. He had been a top performer for a number of years and had been tipped to become a director. He was told to pitch for a project with a large provider of financial services and that would secure him the directorship.

Jeremy said that it wasn't his field and asked for someone else to do it. He was told in a five-minute conversation with a director that this was not an option. Meanwhile, Jeremy's team members were raising concerns about their future as rumours had spread that securing this client would secure the company's future and the alternative might mean redundancies. Two of Jeremy's team members Fran and Michel had experience of financial services pitches. They individually went to talk to Jeremy and asked if they could help with the pitch.

At the same time Jeremy's wife lost her job. Jeremy developed panic attacks. To deal with his anxiety he asserted his control, ran the pitch and tried to avoid letting anyone see how stressed he was by avoiding lengthy individual meetings. Instead, he ran group meetings, barked orders but got the pitch done. He did not take up Fran and Michel on their offer for help in the beginning stages because he didn't give them time to explain how their expertise could help, instead thinking that they might take his job. They both moved to a competitor causing Jeremy's boss to have increasing concerns about his management capacity.

When it came to the pitch, although the financial services firm was happy with the content of Jeremy's pitch, they were not confident they could trust him because he was not open to questions and although he was polite the feedback was that he 'seemed really angry'.

There is no doubt that many relationships in which one party is dependent on the other for money, and potentially survival, can create conflict. Even unknowingly, one party may become resentful of the other person because they feel beholden to them. They may become irritated at the other person for not giving them what they want and need. They may take them for granted and the person who holds the purse strings may unknowingly take advantage of their position of control. This can set up a number of dysfunctional dynamics and conflicts that can affect the future working relationship.

Case study

David was the CEO of a charity which relied on its funding from a local authority department (the 'department') in return for providing mental health support to young people. Tom, the head of the department had a different approach to David in terms of where the service should be headed. David had spoken to a number of other providers and experts in the field who agreed with him and thought that Tom's approach was wrong and that he was going to be putting a number of people at risk. Tom's approach would also mean that David's charity would not receive a grant from the department the following year and would have to dissolve.

David spoke to a number of people about the mistake Tom was making and went into a meeting all guns blazing with Tom to try and convince him that his approach was wrong. Tom said that he was very concerned about awarding David the contract.

David subsequently used the negotiating difficult conversations template. He realised that even though his indignation at Tom's view was justified it was not serving him or his organisation. He went around the conversation differently and was able to negotiate the direction of the contract so that it worked for all parties. In fact he was able to bring Tom around to his point of view. However, he said himself that if he had continued his self-righteous indignation that Tom 'just didn't get it', no matter how justified that may have been, the contract and relationship with the council would have been lost.

The following areas of the audit take the temperature of conflicts as they affect clients and stakeholders and their potential impact:

- Employee questionnaire: Question 12.
- Director/team lead questionnaire: Questions 3 to 6.
- Head of legal/HR/finance questionnaire: Questions 8, 10 to 11, 13 and 14 (time spent on management discussions about conflict could be time not focussing on clients or future business).
- Client/stakeholder questionnaire: Questions 1 to 7.

Maximising the audit's management opportunities

The questionnaires are the beginning of a conversation and so similar principles will need to be followed in taking and following up on the questionnaire as other parts of the early resolution conversation. In particular:

- Confidentiality will allow the respondent to be candid and hopefully provide useful feedback to the organisation
- Post-questionnaire feedback to respondents will be needed to ensure that the respondents know that they have been listened to in the same way as there would need to be in a verbal conversation. This can happen through:
  - implementing employee suggestions
  - providing feedback as to why certain suggestions cannot or should not be followed up on
  - putting forward staged proposals for future working.

Step 3: Build the resolution team

When the decision is taken to introduce, in some form, a set of early resolution interventions or an early resolution scheme, thought will need to be put into the process to make that happen.

The resolution team will include key people who will influence the process of introducing the early resolution scheme and ensure that the messages that sit around it work for the organisation. These will include people who may have the capacity to be conflict coaches and resolution agents. They will also include people who may have the most to gain and lose from the introduction of mediation and early resolution schemes.

The resolution team will include influencers that do not want or are not necessarily convinced about introducing the scheme as well as those who may be more enthusiastic about it.

It is important that this group is not dominated by HR or directors but rather that it provides a good cross-section of members of the organisation. If conflict resolution remains solely the responsibility of HR or high-level decision-makers, it may become very difficult to implement change. This is because individuals may be tempted to revert to the dynamic of HR assuming the parental role of punishing, rewarding and sorting instead of enabling, empowering and facilitating. Levels of trust and openness will not change and those in conflict will not be enabled to take responsibility for the situations in which they find themselves.

The resolution team will play an important role in communicating about and championing key aspects of the early resolution scheme. Each layer of the organisation and team within it will have its own language and its own culture. So, it will be really important for the different languages and cultures of the organisation to be heard and spoken to through the resolution scheme. The resolution team will be key 'translators' in that process.

The resolution team will be led by the resolution lead who feels confident to apply the principles throughout the process of setting up the team. Ideally, they will have undergone mediation or conflict resolution skills training and their ability to demonstrate the skills will be crucial to successful implementation.

Most important in choosing the team will be to ensure that it represents a cross-section of the organisation. This may include:

- team leaders
- motivated employees
- disruptive employees
- directors
- HR
- union representatives.

Bringing together this team will be an important step in rethinking hierarchy in an organisation as it applies to conflict resolution. It will introduce a culture in which everyone within the organisation is empowered to be responsible for effective conflict resolution and where one individual can conflict coach or mentor another notwithstanding their position in the organisation. This will not take away from the discipline, structure and performance targets of the organisation. Rather, it will enable all members of the organisation to be equipped to work through conflict and in so doing be motivated to improving organisational and individual efficiency and wellbeing.

In old-fashioned hierarchical structures, placing resolution agents at all levels of the organisation may have seemed or been impossible. However, in modern organisations it becomes increasingly possible for different levels of the organisation to lead on this new type of initiative for a variety of reasons:

- Younger members of the organisation will often be quite adept and well adjusted to conflict coaching and mentoring concepts having learnt them in the context of the modern schooling system making it a part of their language.
- More people are returning to work or restarting careers which means you may have 'junior' members of staff who may have more life experience than senior members.
- Younger members of staff sometimes have more technical experience than their elders, particularly in the digital arena.
- As increasing value is placed on emotional intelligence, individuals become more open to learn from others notwithstanding their position or age.

Step 4: Develop capacity for SOUL-based conversations

Introducing an early resolution scheme and making these decisions means starting a new way of having conversations straightaway. The way that the early resolution team makes decisions about the scheme will then be more easily replicated in other areas of the organisation where group decisions need to be made in terms of reaching agreement and dealing with disagreement. On the basis of what we have discussed already, the aim is that this approach will have the following outcomes:

- **Self-aware conversations** in which individuals take responsibility for their actions and decisions.
- **Opportunities** to rebuild relationships and create alternatives.
- **Understanding** of our own and each other's positions, motivations and drivers.
- **Learning** replaces blame and shame.

These SOUL-based conversations will start with conversations between the resolution lead and the members of the resolution team to:

- identify the key areas of resistance – 'Mediation doesn't feel safe' or 'We don't want to give staff an inch for them to take a mile.'
- identify common areas of generic low-level dissatisfaction or resentment within the organisation
- identify areas for facilitation or negotiation between key groups including key ground rules
- review mechanisms to deal with non-agreement
- review mechanisms to carry agreement through to be reflected in future action.

By the very nature of the make-up of the resolution team and the fact that there will be change, conflict may present itself within the team itself. The conflicts that arise will be great indicators of the general feelings within the business and a great place to start the process of implementing the early resolution culture.

Even if there is a good business case for an early resolution scheme, there will not necessarily be a good level of trust between the representative groups. For example, some individuals may see the move towards using mediation as a ploy by management to reduce costs and get people out of the company quietly. Others may be concerned that mediation does not guarantee a clear result or that it may create more opportunities to complain. HR may be concerned that by passing the matter to the mediator, they risk losing control of the conflict and so management of the organisation's people. They may also be concerned that the changes threaten their position within the organisation or will impose more work pressure.

There will be a number of concerns that we have not even considered. These will all be valid responses and will be reflected, in some way, throughout the organisation so they need to be addressed systematically.

Underlying concerns for individual members of the guiding team may include:

- Is this going to open the door to more complaining?
- If people start talking negatively about the way I manage, will I be exposed or undermined?
- If mediation is introduced will my job become redundant?
- Will all this talking about the problem give me a number of new problems?

The answer to all of these questions is definitely . . . maybe. Addressing conflict can mean going into the eye of the storm because it is only in identifying the problems that solutions can be found. It is very important, however, to remember that if the conflict or issue is there it is not going to go away and if it is not addressed, the most likely route it is going to take is escalation which will necessarily affect the rest of the organisation.

The reason that most of us avoid conflict generally comes down to our fears. Some of those fears have been highlighted already in this book and some may be difficult to discern or be based on feelings or perspectives rather than fact. The fact remains that if we are not equipped to address some of these fears and change through conflict, it is likely that we will leave ourselves vulnerable with more problems.

Identifying some of the concerns of the guiding team starts to highlight the realities of some of the challenges within the organisation. In my experience these have included:

- Low-level but long-standing resentments about the way management communicates with staff and how things are said and done.

- The manner in which HR is engaged with situations and then overridden by director decisions or undermined in some other way.

- Lack of organisational infrastructure, whether in terms of its existence or its implementation – 'Even if we resolve this how can we guarantee that anything will be done about it?'

SOUL-based conversations create a holding room to contain those fears and concerns and see and address the presenting issues honestly and safely. The solutions then have room to emerge and can include the following:

- Instead of your job becoming redundant your skills may need to change and this could open up new opportunities and, at the very least, new skill sets.

- Sometimes, the only way I am going to change what I am doing is by other people telling me, and my coming to the conclusion that what I am doing is not working. It is only then that I can start seeing the alternatives.

- Talking about the problem will clarify its various strands. It may expose issues that I have not seen or talked about before but by exposing them I have the opportunity to see them and systematically address them.

- We need to find ways to work together differently.

Step 5: Embrace potential obstacles

Asking members of the resolution team to identify the potential obstacles from their representative group is a great way to both obtain a generic idea of the issues and obstacles that are and can be faced within the organisation. It also bottoms out the concerns that the leaders of your guiding team may have, but may be reluctant to take ownership of, for whatever reason. Very similar to the mediation process this step allows for venting, judgement and criticism of each other and the organisation. It's an opportunity to bring things out in the open and in so doing both identify the action points and flush out the myths.

Step 6: Learn from history

Identifying and beginning to deal with historic conflicts within the group, which will more than likely be affecting other change processes within the organisation, will provide an opportunity to turn around the messages that have sat alongside these conflicts and resolve them. This would be through conflict coaching and potentially mediating with or between individuals within the resolution team who are found to have low-level but long-standing resentments with respect to other members of the team or the organisation itself.

It is important to manage this process very carefully and that this process is carried out by a mediator or individual experienced in dealing with conflict. The way individuals and their concerns are managed in this process will affect the way the introduction of conflict resolution is viewed and of how you 'walk the walk'. The management of this process plants the seed for the early resolution programme and gives the key influencers first-hand experience of how it works.

Step 7: Implement the early resolution scheme framework

This stage in the process focusses on providing a functioning structure in which the early resolution scheme can work in practice. This will need to be tailored to the process and messaging of each particular organisation and this section is not intended to provide a definitive solution but rather a framework around which processes and solutions can be hung.

Create the early resolution scheme infrastructure

The early resolution scheme infrastructure concentrates on having the right people at the relevant touch points to identify and support with conflicts. How the infrastructure is set up will vary from one organisation to another but will include key roles that may already exist within the organisation.

Mentors

Mentors are often used as guides to enable performance, particularly at the early stages. Assigning each employee at any level with a mentor can be a key tool to turn conflict around at an early stage, no matter the size or infrastructure of the organisation. It can help the organisation to do the following:

- Clarify, explain and reinforce key organisational messages, values and expectations.
- Identify key areas of concern.
- Pre-empt potential conflict at an early stage.

And it can help the individual to do the following:

- Understand the expectations of the organisation.
- Understand what the individual can expect from the organisation.
- Raise and address low-level concerns.
- Talk through the options and how the organisation can and cannot address them when sticky situations come up.

Personal conflict coaches

The personal conflict coach may also be a mentor. However, their role will be specifically to support and enable the person they are conflict coaching (the coachee) to achieve their goals and aspirations in relation to the conflict situation or more generally. This will not be about showing them what they need to do to succeed within the organisation as this prescriptive guidance will be provided by the mentor. Rather, the conflict coach will provide the coachee with an opportunity to discuss and make decisions about what they are doing in the organisation in the context of the bigger picture, namely the other factors that are important to them in their lives.

The coachee may feel that because the mentor has been communicating key messages of the organisation they are not as independent as they could be and so may need someone else to act as their conflict coach depending on the organisation's capacity.

The key to make the conflict coach role most effective is that the coachee trusts that the coach is impartial. This is particularly important to enable conversations in which the coachee's goals seem to conflict with those of the organisation. The coaching conversation can create a valuable opportunity to work through those conflicts of interest and often provide opportunities for the employee to choose an alignment of interest.

Case study

Mitesh built apps for a successful financial technology company that was rapidly expanding. He had worked for the company for three years and had created a number of successful products. However, the director he reported to had made a number of comments about his recent lateness and had asked him to attend a formal performance meeting.

Before the performance meeting with his manager, Mitesh had a conversation with a conflict coach. He said that he was turning up late because he was unmotivated as he felt that he was building the product but had no ownership of the company and he was considering setting up in competition with the company. During the course of the conflict coaching conversation, Mitesh realised that he really liked the company but wanted more ownership. Initially he thought that he had the following options: to leave the company and set up in competition, to demand a share of the company or to threaten to leave and see if the company gave him what he wanted.

However, after talking the situation through with the conflict coach he realised he needed to:

- tell his boss that he realised that he had been turning up late and that was not working for the company
- admit that he had felt unmotivated and wanted more ownership of the business
- acknowledge that if the company were to give him more ownership they would probably want to see more commitment and better timekeeping
- improve his timekeeping
- ask for what he wanted in terms of share of ownership
- be prepared to negotiate
- look at alternative options.

Because Mitesh came to these realisations, there were no shocks for either side and both the company and Mitesh were able to negotiate and make measured decisions without having to make threats. In this case, Mitesh did leave the company. However, because the conversations had been honest and amicable and he had been supported through the conflict coaching relationship, Mitesh kept in touch with the conflict coach and other members of the organisation and came back to become a director and shareholder with the company some years later.

Resolution agents

The role of the resolution agent has been set out in Chapter 8 as a managerial role in which the manager informally mediates according to the principles. It will be important that the resolution agent stays clear to their brief particularly in terms of impartiality and retaining confidentiality. If the resolution agent is also a conflict coach, it will be necessary for them to have either coached both or neither of the parties in the dispute. This is so that they can remain 'omnipartial' – on the side of both parties, and ensure that they have the trust and confidence of the parties.

Internal mediators

Whether the organisation trains internal mediators will depend on the organisation's priorities. It is worth noting that the path to becoming a mediator can be incremental, building on personal conflict coaching skills to becoming an accredited mediator, as well as the effectiveness of early resolution approaches.

In any event there are advantages and disadvantages to having internal mediators as shown below.

Challenges associated with internal mediators	Advantages of internal mediators
- Buy-in by the parties as internal mediators can be seen as being partial - Mediating and ongoing continual professional development can take the internal mediator away from their day job - The frequency with which the mediator can mediate may be limited - There is need for clarity on when and whether to refer to external mediators	- They lead early resolution culture including training, managing mentoring feedback and supporting the peer coaches and resolution agents with continuing professional development - Where the organisation is spread over multiple sites, the internal mediator can be truly impartial by virtue of not knowing the parties - Cross-organisational resolution schemes can be operated in which organisations provide and use each other's mediators

External mediators

There may be external mediators available who will be fully independent of the organisation. Even with this independence, the parties will still need to trust that the mediator is on their side. If mediation is agreed between the parties, the organisation should propose an internal mediator or mediation organisation to the parties. They should be able to ask for a choice of up to three mediators and have a confidential discussion with the mediator before deciding whether to go ahead or not.

Mediation coordinator

The mediation coordinator will ideally be a member of the resolution team and in all likelihood will be a member of the HR team. The mediation coordinator will help to set up the mediation or work through what the options will be for the parties if one of them does not want to mediate. For this reason, it is very helpful for them to be trained in mediation skills as they will effectively be conflict coaching the parties to make a decision about whether or not to mediate. If the parties subsequently require advice on formal processes, the mediation coordinator can refer them to a member of the HR team.

Step 8: Create processes and policies

The process used by organisations will depend on the size and existing structures of the organisation. Because the early resolution scheme by its nature needs a level of flexibility, it is helpful to introduce an early resolution policy with guidelines that are cross-referenced to the organisation's other employment policies and documents. Any such policy will also need due consultation.

How the policies and processes are worded will depend on what is already in place and will require thought on a case-by-case basis. Some people call this a mediation scheme but widening it to an Early Resolution and Mediation Scheme highlights that mediation is not the only answer and allows for conflicts to be addressed early with the appropriate touchpoints.

Suggested elements for inclusion in policies and contractual documents are set out below.

Early resolution and mediation policy

This policy introduces and explains how, when and why mediation can be used and accessed in the organisation as well as the benefits to the employee.

Early resolution and mediation policy

Introduction

[Organisation] is committed to a proactive approach to resolving the conflicts that can arise at work at an early stage and in a way that works for everyone. Throughout the organisation, [mentors], [personal conflict coaches], [resolution agents] [and mediators] are available to help you work through difficult conversations, negotiations or encounters you may be having with your colleagues in confidence. In certain cases, mediation may be a suitable option as an alternative or in addition to the formal grievance procedures available to you.

Policy aims

- To provide individuals with an alternative, impartial, non-judgemental framework to address and resolve conflicts to the satisfaction of all involved.

- To provide a framework which helps to improve empowered communication throughout the organisation.

- To offer alternatives to a formal grievance to resolve issues.

If you feel that you need help with resolving an issue with a colleague you can contact the following people IN CONFIDENCE who will either help you personally or refer you to someone else who can:

MENTOR COORDINATOR [name]

Mentors are people who know the organisation and its values well and are here to help you progress in your current position.

CONFLICT COACH COORDINATOR [name]

Conflict coaches are here if you need a confidential discussion about a particular problem or issue you are experiencing. They will help you to be clear on what you want to happen in that situation and help you move towards that.

RESOLUTION AGENTS [names]

Resolution agents can help facilitate conversations between you and individuals you are having trouble communicating with. Resolution agents may be people who work with or manage you but will be trained to support you to resolve the matter fairly.

IN-HOUSE MEDIATORS [names]

In-house mediators will take you through our in-house mediation process for conflict situations you are experiencing with colleagues. Discussions with in-house mediators will be confidential unless otherwise agreed between you and them. Also, mediation with an in-house mediator is a voluntary process which you and your colleagues would need to agree to entering into. In-house mediators are necessarily impartial and work to help both parties involved.

EXTERNAL MEDIATORS [names]

External mediators are available to help you mediate between your colleagues and the company if necessary. Discussions with external mediators will be confidential unless you decide that specific information needs to be disclosed. Also, mediation with an external mediator is a voluntary process which you and your colleagues would need to agree to entering into. External mediators are impartial and totally independent of the company and not on one side or the other

MEDIATION COORDINATOR [name]

The mediation coordinator will help you set up a mediation or help you work through what to do if the other person does not want to mediate.

HR

The HR department can help you with any mediation, grievance or disciplinary process. If you are currently in a grievance or disciplinary process, you can consider using any of the alternatives set out in this scheme at the same time.

If you want to mediate the matter, you should contact [] to identify:

● alternative solutions to mediation if appropriate

● in-house mediation

● referral to an external mediation provider.

EARLY RESOLUTION POLICY FAQs

What is mediation?

Mediation is a **voluntary, confidential process** in which an **impartial** third party supports the parties to come to a solution that works for them without giving advice or opinions.

What should I expect to happen in a mediation?

When both parties have agreed to mediate, a date will be set for the mediation to happen. The mediator will speak to both parties before that date to understand what has been going on for them and what they want from the process.

How long?

The mediation will take between half a day and a day although in certain cases it may last up to two days.

What happens?

The mediation meetings will consist of face-to-face meetings and private meetings with the mediator depending on what the mediator considers will be most efficient and effective. At the end of the mediation, you may come to an agreement. You will also need to agree what part of that agreement you share with other individuals and/or the organisation and what you will keep confidential and the mediator will help you do that.

Do I have to mediate?

Because mediation is a voluntary process, you do not have to mediate. It is worth having a confidential conversation with the mediator or a conflict coach to talk through the potential advantages and disadvantages of mediating before making a final decision so that your decision is well thought through.

Can I make the other person mediate?

As above, mediation is a voluntary process so no one can be forced into it. However, you can encourage the other person to speak to the mediator in confidence before they make a final decision as to whether to mediate or not.

How does the help available through the early resolution scheme, including mediation, fit with the formal grievance and disciplinary processes?

Generally, options available through the early resolution scheme can be used at any stage although the organisation may need to impose boundaries on that depending on resources available. If the parties choose to mediate, any grievance will be put on hold while the mediation takes place.

What happens if I want to mediate?

If you feel comfortable, it is always helpful to talk through the issue first with a conflict coach or resolution agent. If you have already done this or don't feel comfortable doing this you can send a request to the mediation coordinator at [] who will then follow the early resolution and mediation procedure.

Contractual provisions

Part of the success of early resolution, as has already been emphasised, is its voluntary nature. When we choose to mediate, we are making an empowered decision to do something about the situation that we find ourselves in. So, it is important to keep to this spirit in the employment contract. Rather than saying, for example, that the parties will mediate, the obligation needs to be for the parties to consider mediation, allowing them to review the situation as it arises rather than feeling forced into facing the other party in situations where that may feel unsafe.

The contractual provisions will need to cover disputes over the contract where there may be a parting of the ways of the individual from the organisation, which I have referred to as 'Employment disputes', and situations where there are disagreements during the course of work between colleagues which I have referred to as 'Workplace disputes'.

Provision for employment disputes

'If any dispute, complaint or disagreement arises relating to this employment contract, the parties will consider resolving it by mediation in accordance with the company's Early Resolution and Mediation Policy. Unless otherwise agreed between the parties, the mediation service provider, [the Conflict Resolution Centre], will nominate a mediator. Mediation is a confidential process and will be entered into both voluntarily and in good faith, and neither party by entering into such a process waives other legal rights.'

Provision for workplace disputes

'If any conflict, disagreement or complaint arises between employees during employment, the parties will consider resolving it by individual conflict coaching and/or mediation in accordance with the company's Early Resolution and Mediation Policy. In order to trigger mediation, the matter should first be referred to the mediation coordinator (as stated in the company's Mediation and Early

> Resolution Policy). Unless otherwise agreed between the
> parties, the mediation service provider, [the Conflict
> Resolution Centre], will nominate the mediator. Media-
> tion is a confidential process and will be entered into
> voluntarily and in good faith, and neither party by
> entering into such a process waives their respective
> statutory or other legal rights.'

Recourse to mediation can also be referred to in grievance, diversity, anti-bullying, harassment and whistle-blowing policies which can include a provision as shown here.

> If either the employee or manager considers that the
> matter might be best resolved through mediation they
> should refer the matter to the mediation coordinator.
> Participating in mediation will not preclude employees
> from taking or continuing with alternative measures as
> set out in the company's grievance procedure if the
> mediation does not resolve the matter.

The disciplinary and capability procedure can also provide recourse to mediation if agreed between the parties. This may need to include a timeframe to avoid prolonged delays in the process.

Early resolution and mediation procedure

The early resolution and mediation process will need to be tailored in accordance with the organisation's policies, procedures and cultures, while ensuring that the process remains as informal and light touch as possible. The table below, sets out how each touch point in the early resolution and mediation process can be used according to how the conflict escalates. It is worth noting that we can often see the escalation of conflict and the movement from conflict coaching to formal mediation as a failure. In fact, the escalation of the conflict can be part of the journey to resolving it and getting to the core of the problem.

Stages of conflict	Opportunity	Early resolution processes	Standard grievance and disciplinary processes
Entrenched conflict between individual and organisation	Dignified separation of ways and opportunity for closure and/or future working	External mediator appointed with legal representation from both parties	Escalation to ACAS / tribunal
Entrenched conflict between individuals	Individuals find a solution and opportunities for new ways of working	External mediator appointed through HR	Grievance and disciplinary action including investigation progresses
		In-house mediation	Grievance / disciplinary action
Early stage conflict _____ Pre-conflict	Individuals can work through specific conflict situations and devise a strategy for their resolution	Resolution agent conducts an informal facilitation / mediation in line with the 7 principles	Matter raised with HR / formal meeting to review the issues
		Peer coach(es) support(s) individual(s) to clarify wants and needs and identify next steps	Matter raised with manager
	From initial engagement, clear messages are communicated between the organisation and individuals about: expectations, responsibilities and how to get help	Mentoring feedback forums	Induction programme

Management of the mediation process

The most sensible place for this process to be managed is through the designated mediation coordinator who is often also a member of the HR team. Two slightly different processes will need to be managed.

- **Workplace mediation:** This will be a less formal form of mediation between individuals who are likely to continue in a working relationship. This type of mediation will focus more on building relationships and boundaries than negotiating the ending of relationship. The mediator also may be a member of the organisation.

● **Employment mediation:** This is likely to be a slightly more formal format of mediation. This will apply to situations where there has been a relationship breakdown and some of the mediation may relate to negotiations and agreements to resolve the issue, and in many cases to part ways. In an employment mediation, the mediator will not be a member of the organisation and lawyers may also need to be present to advise the parties on consequences of the decisions they are making in the mediation. The matter may also have been escalated to court or tribunal. The process for employment mediation is discussed in more detail in Part 3.

In workplace mediation, the process will normally play out as follows.

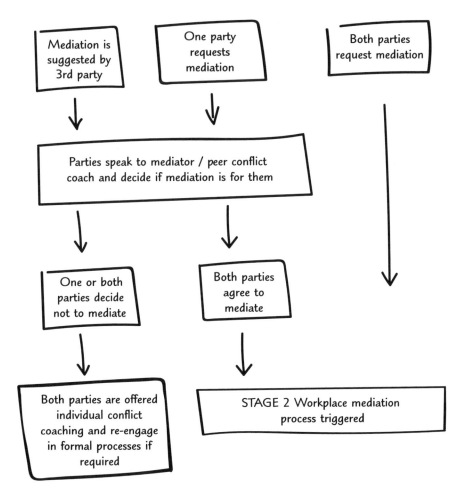

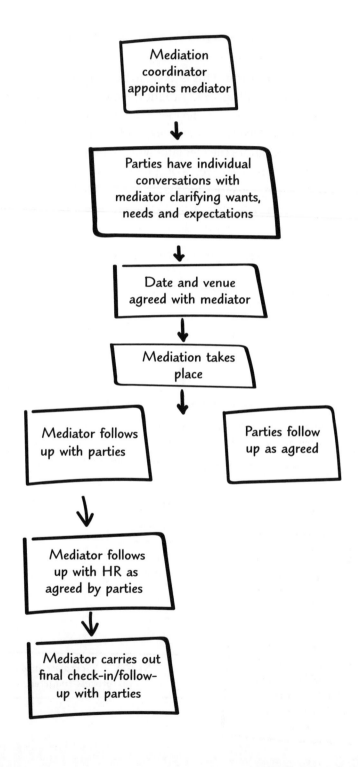

Step 9: Develop the learning environment

Education is the most powerful weapon you can use to change the world

Nelson Mandela

Any early resolution scheme will rely on continuous professional development for it to work. Particularly with respect to our knowledge on personal development, most of us forget what we learn the next day and we give up on positive intentions much faster than we would wish. Eighty percent of New Year's Resolutions fail by February (https://health.usnews.com/health-news/blogs/eat-run/articles/2015-12-29/why-80-percent-of-new-years-resolutions-fail) so the learning environment is crucial to keep people on track in terms of the whys and hows of early resolution.

The process of professional development will also help to filter who is best suited to which roles as follows.

> Train the resolution team together with relevant management and HR in basic early resolution skills

> Establish from training appetite and suitability for peer coach, resolution agents and mediation roles

Most conflict resolution and mediation training programmes can be cumulative, meaning that it can be relatively easy for a conflict coach to move to becoming a resolution agent and subsequently a mediator. It also allows the organisation to gauge the benefit of early resolution interventions without making unnecessary or unproven financial commitments.

Step 1O: Develop and communicate key messages

Ideally, the use of mediation and early resolution tools should be integrated and talked about as part of the organisation's culture. This is preferable to it being something that employees have to search for in a policy when the issue has escalated. It is helpful for information about process and how to seek help in the midst of difficult conversations and conflict to be communicated in as light a way as possible. This is most effective when done through the resolution team who will champion the early resolution and mediation scheme and messages associated with them.

Clarify the message

Key decisions will need to be made as part of the process of introducing the early resolution scheme so that the scheme messages are clear and easily understood. These decisions will include the following:

- Whether to introduce the various roles ranging from mentor to mediator into the organisation.
- Which roles, if any, will not be included.
- Who to place in those roles.
- How to integrate those roles into other roles within the organisation (for example, adding conflict coaching to existing coaches skills).
- What levels of professional development for employees and members of the resolution team will be required,
- How to reconcile 'the day job' with all levels of the organisation in the early resolution process.

Communicate the message

The most effective way of communicating the message of early resolution will be through the resolution team. Through the process of devising and implementing the scheme they will have been able to experience the benefits. It is also helpful to communicate the message in more conventional ways letting people know that there are alternatives available. The form of words for a poster below is one way of communicating the message.

Are relationships at work making you

anxious, stressed or uneasy?

Mediation or conflict coaching is available to help you:

- talk things through in a confidential, safe environment
- work out what you want to do about the situation
- find a resolution
- work out how to move forward

Contact . . . to find out more

Early resolution in schools

Building early resolution schemes in schools can have a wide-reaching impact on the young people but it will also influence their families and communities. The starting point for this is identifying the benefits and integrating the skills. The most effective way of doing this is by teaching the teachers to model the skills with young people and where appropriate use them in difficult situations with parents. It then extends to teaching young people the skills to resolve conflict early which has benefits that go beyond the resolution of conflicts because it develops leadership capacity and communication skills.

Once young people learn early conflict resolution skills, they can start to feel empowered simply through using them and starting to own them. Equally, giving the young people the skills to support each other through conflict situations provides an opportunity to receive a truly empathetic response from someone who can really understand. As they see issues between their parents and teachers resolved in this way, it can provide a model for them to use to resolve their own challenges.

Teenagers have a unique ability to communicate and understand each other. Because the prefrontal cortex is still developing, they might rely on a part of the brain called the amygdala to make decisions and solve problems more than adults do. The amygdala is associated with emotions, impulses, aggression and instinctive behaviour. These are the kind of reactions that adults are more prone to having in more acute conflict situations. Because of this, conflict over what we might view as silly or trivial occur often or are more obvious in teenage life. By acknowledging this and giving young people the tools at the age of eight or nine to address and support each other in day-to-day conflicts, we are providing them with a foundation they will be able to use throughout their life. In this way, the young people stop being the problem and start becoming the solution.

The intensity of puberty including the pre-pubescent stage and adolescence essentially renders young people experts in conflict. They can use that to their advantage by becoming increasingly equipped to empathise with others in conflict situations, to normalise as opposed to dramatise conflict in some ways and to go through a process to deal with it. What is more, young people are deemed to be able to learn things more easily (see research by Nigel Emptage of University of Oxford) and so may be less resistant to learning different responses to conflict than adults. By providing young people with the skills to manage themselves in these situations, they start to teach and inform adults who are not always so adept at dealing with these situations either.

Case study

I was teaching a group of 13 year olds expansive listening skills including summarising and paraphrasing in line with Step 11 of the resolution framework. One girl Alexa was practising the skills with Billie. Initially, Alexa said she couldn't paraphrase and summarise because it was too hard.

I demonstrated what I had heard Billie saying along the lines of 'What I understood was that Billie wanted to do well but she was resistant to doing her homework because her mum was nagging her.' Billie said 'Yes, kind of', Alexa chipped in and said, 'No, she was saying that she needs someone to help her with her homework but she doesn't want her mum to help her — she wants her friend to help her because her mum doesn't understand.'

This case study demonstrates that although I was an expert in dealing with conflict, it was much more effective for the young people who could relate to their peer to listen, and in so doing get to the root of the problem and the potential solution.

Developing capacity for empathy and mutual understanding

Research shows that we cannot expect a child or teenager to develop the capacity for empathy unless they have been on the receiving end of repeated empathetic responses from a significant adult over time (read more in the book 'Bothered: Helping Teenagers Talk About Their Feelings' by Margot Sutherland). So, any process of teaching empathy needs also to ensure that the child or teenager we are trying to teach feels that they are being empathised with first. This also emphasises the benefits of teaching young people to effectively empathise with each other simply because it is easier to do so when they are going through similar experiences

Building confidence

When young people can see their value and how they contribute in society, it can immediately increase their confidence and perspective on what they are capable of. Teaching young people how to empower each other through reflective listening can achieve this because they immediately see the relief or joy of the other person when they have been heard or understood. They can also see how they can and have made a difference in helping them to sort out their problem and demonstrate to themselves skills that they didn't know they had. This can give the young person an augmented sense of self that can be thrilling.

Case study

When Sasha started the conflict coaching sessions she remained silent throughout the initial sessions. She was very reluctant to contribute to the class discussions or to share any part of her experience.

In the session that covered paraphrasing and summarising she practised the skills with her partner. She quite quickly got the hang of using the skills and saw very clearly how using the skills enabled the girl she was conflict coaching to talk through the situation and find a resolution to it.

She reported that she also felt more confident to say what she thought as she said she knew that if she was in a conflict with someone she would know how to sort it out.

Developing negotiation skills

Young people generally have a good set of negotiation skills. Often we as parents teach them these skills. A child will ask for a Halloween outfit and we may say that we will buy them accessories for their existing outfit. Or, we might ask them to do their homework and they might respond 'If I do my homework can I have a sweet.' Bribery or negotiation, call it what you will, kids at an early stage learn to negotiate in the course of pushing boundaries.

Often we do not want to value kids for these skills as they are challenging for parents and teachers to deal with. However, they are extremely valuable skills. Teaching young people about different ways in which they can negotiate can be really exciting for them because they immediately see that if they negotiate better they are more likely to get what they want.

It can also start to demonstrate that people have limits and they need to manage their own expectations around those limits. Once young people understand that negotiation can be a structured process, and if they are good at it they might get more of what they want, they start to become more interested in how it works. In particular, they start to understand how to ask for what they want, understand what they are unlikely to get and, crucially, feel valued for skills that may previously be deemed to be naughty or annoying. In this way, young people can start to be comfortable with respecting other people's boundaries while boosting their own self-esteem.

Creating the early resolution scheme framework

As with a workplace early resolution scheme, systems or solutions set up within the school, university or college environment, will need to work with existing policies and initiatives. Crucially, any scheme will need to pay careful attention to child protection and health and safety issues particularly where students are coaching or mentoring each other. This can be addressed at least in part by telling the students that during the course of any early resolution conversation, that information indicating that a young person may be at risk will always need to be divulged. Systems will also need to ensure that young people are at all times supported and are not caused to feel or be over-responsible for their peers.

Equip teachers with conflict coaching skills

It is important that key messages relating to early resolution are modelled by teachers. In particular, teachers will need to be equipped to have conversations that focus on listening as opposed to telling. This can be tricky in establishing discipline as setting rules and boundaries in the classroom are essential to ensuring structure and safety.

So, thought will need to go to making particular space or time to taking some conversations or challenging scenarios outside the frame of the classroom and into an environment with less time and attention pressures. At these times, teachers will need to be equipped to use and model the key listening skills and SOUL-based conversations we have covered.

Identify and train conflict coaching leads

Conflict coaching leads are students who have trained in personal conflict coaching skills and who can practise them with their peers. This will probably work in the context of other schemes and buddying systems. Alternatively, these may be skills provided by anti-bullying champions.

Provide a feedback system to conflict coaching leads

Crucial to an effective conflict coaching system will be careful consideration of child protection issues as has been mentioned. It will also be important to ensure that the conflict coaching lead is supported and has back-up. Like any coach, they will need to debrief and work through situations that did not go well or as expected. Generally this works well in facilitated forums or coaching clubs.

Provide a model for reception staff, PTA leads and governors to address difficult conversations

This may seem like a tall order as it may be difficult to coordinate time and justify the spending of that time. However, this type of training can be light touch and provide a model to cope with and deal with conversations while ensuring that key messages and feedback are not lost.

The following model is suggested as an initial response to parents who are upset with something at school and need support. Clearly schools need to be careful about what and how they communicate. The suggestion below will need to be adapted to each school or headteacher's style. It is also unlikely to be an any written form. However, the wording below can be useful in setting the tone and communicating key messages. It is also clear any communication of an early resolution model will include recourse to appropriate individuals for support including the class teacher, head of year and headteacher as appropriate.

Guidelines for speaking to parents

Often when parents raise issues, they are understandably fraught with emotion and it can be difficult to fully understand the problem for the parent and the issues surrounding it. These issues are also sometimes raised at times where there are time pressures such as between drop-off and work and so we can be or feel in a hurry to deal with them and find a solution.

Staff or parents may feel frustrated with the way the parent is dealing with the situation and may instinctively want to brush them off. However, this approach often escalates the situation and can exacerbate it with parents feeling unheard, angry and concerned that their issue is not going to be dealt with, resulting, for example, in their child having a difficult day at school that day. So initially:

- Identify what the big picture is or what is the parent really asking for?
- Know your limitations
- Communicate only what you can do:
  - What I can do is . . .
  - If you want Y then you need to speak to . . .

Setting boundaries and looking after ourselves

When someone comes up to us in the playground, we can jump into trying to help them because we can see how

---

important the issue is to the parent. However, we can sometimes start to try to help at a time when we are not able to really support the individual involved: we may need to go to work or be rushing to an appointment, we may be thinking or worrying about our own child.

Rather than helping the situation, that individual is likely to feel more unheard and more frustrated. There is no point pretending to be there for someone if it is not a good time for us. If we do this we will often be less equipped to help them and may exacerbate the situation in trying to deal with it at that time.

Rather, it can be helpful to set up a time to talk about it and to set up a boundary around that time to ensure that it doesn't run on unnecessarily and is manageable in the context of your own day.

Ask yourself:

- Do I have the time/emotional capacity to deal with this issue right now?
- What is this issue triggering for me?
- What do I need to do to look after myself?

Ask the parent if they have five minutes to talk about this now or over the phone at a better time?

<u>Adopting expansive listening and questioning techniques</u>

When you have fixed an appropriate time or in an appropriate environment to have a conversation with the parent, paying attention to your listening and questioning can help.

Step 1: Listen

The easiest way to diffuse or breathe some air into the situation is through listening and crucially seeking to understand before we seek to respond. When listening, we will use the key tools of empathy, summarising, paraphrasing and silent listening. We can then ask ourselves if we have really heard the parent and whether we can disassociate our judgement of what they have said from what they have said. If the parent keeps repeating the same thing it may be that we have not really heard them, or in any event, that they do not feel heard. In these cases we can reflect back, saying: 'You keep on repeating the fact that . . . and so it sounds like this is really important to you.' This acknowledges that you know it is a problem for them and that it is important but also that you do not necessarily have a solution to it and that it remains their issue to resolve although you want to help them if you can.

Step 2: What do they want and how are they going to get it?

Particularly when acting as someone who is not necessarily going to be able to find a definitive solution to the problem, use open questions – What, How, Where, Which, Who. We can employ the GROW model (for problem-solving and goal-setting) to help them work out what they need to do personally and where they need to ask for help.

Step 3: Ask if they want your opinion

When people approach us with a problem, we assume they want us to give them a solution and to tell them what we think, but this is often not the case. Rather, they (and we!) want an opportunity to talk through the situation and be told they are right. In these circumstances, where we want to help and fix but the help is not wanted, we can often give away really useful information and find that it can fall on deaf ears or is treated with hostility. That can sour our relationship and create an additional problem.

A much more positive way of dealing with this situation is to ask the individual if they want our opinion. Once they know you have an opinion they will want to know what it is. When presented in this way they are much more likely to listen to it. Equally, they can be clear that they do not want to hear our opinion. When expressed in this way, we can be clear that this is only an opinion about what they could do as opposed to a judgement of what they should do. It is also a reminder to ourselves that we do not have all the answers.

Step 4: Follow-up

In situations that relate to issues with children, emotions run high and parents or carers generally want an acknowledgement that they are supported in a difficult situation. So, follow-up is a powerful way to demonstrate that you have not forgotten that they have told you about the issue and that it was important to you although you cannot necessarily fix it.

It also allows you to ensure that the issue has not been dropped if actions are needed to be taken around it. This kind of follow-up can be introduced in a light way by saying something like 'Do you have a minute?' or 'How is it going?'

Early resolution in the community

Social capital is defined by the Organisation for Economic Cooperation and Development (OECD) as 'networks together with shared norms, values and understandings that facilitate co-operation within or among groups'. Or it can be described as the value that the quantity and quality of social relations can have on our happiness and our success. In other words, the better we engage with our communities and peers, the happier and more successful we and our communities are likely to be.

This means that the value of nurturing and developing communities translates into social capital as an essential component of economic development (for more read *Is Social Capital Declining in the United States?* by Pamela Paxton). Crucially, it is also among the most important determinants of happiness (see *Happiness: Transforming the Development Landscape* relating to Bhutan and *Social Capital and Individual Happiness in Europe* by Andres Rodriguez Pose and Viola von Berlepsch).

There are clearly various points at which social capital becomes threatened, particularly when relationships or community ties break down or the norms and understandings that facilitate cooperation change. This can happen at the level of disagreements between neighbours who may formerly have been friends but can no longer look at each other because of noise issues between their properties. It can break down where local councils are at odds with local charities, providers and suppliers. The result can be a breakdown in communication between decision-makers and communities, a feeling of alienation, a lack of specific and general group understanding, as well as gang or sectarian violence.

Building and sustaining relationships between communities can go a long way to developing those communities' social capital. In order to build and create community cohesion, key individuals or touch points will need to be identified to model and practise the principles of early conflict resolution. This is likely to be a looser model than in schools and in organisations but is workable nevertheless. In order to build early resolution systems in the community, the following steps need to be taken.

Identify the resolution team

The first step is to identify key posts and individuals across the community who come across conflict regularly and have an understanding of sources of conflict within the community. These will include:

- housing association contact points
- community groups and umbrella bodies for those groups
- religious and spiritual groups
- primary care providers and community groups
- school leaders
- business leaders and entrepreneurs
- local authority representatives
- gang leaders
- parents
- council members
- politicians.

The core resolution team will come out of these groups and may be self-selecting as they learn more about the value and options for early resolution. The more representative these individuals are of the various factions of the community, the easier it will be to address presenting issues and create forums for building empathy and understanding within the community. For example, gang leaders are likely to push back against and not trust police officers who want to resolve their disputes. However, introducing individuals who are or have been gang members creates a platform in which honest discussions can start to happen. Nobody wants to see their friend killed in gang violence and that violence only generally happens because people can see no other option. A resolution agent trusted in that environment can start to open up the options and build trust.

Demonstrate the value of early resolution and options for engagement

In some cases, the groups or individuals within the groups listed above will be hard to reach and slow to trust. Because of this, any intervention needs to demonstrate an impact and an opportunity for the individuals to take ownership and control. There are various potential points of engagement which can help build trust and options for early resolution.

Restorative justice

Restorative justice (RJ) is a process in which victims have the opportunity to meet or communicate with the perpetrator of the crime to explain the impact it had on them. It also provides an opportunity for offenders to take responsibility and make amends. It has been demonstrated that £8 is saved for every £1 spent on restorative justice and there are benefits in both reductions in reoffending and in providing tangible benefits to victims (see the House of Commons Justice Committee Fourth Report of Session 2016–17).

Accessibility of RJ may be patchy and will be reliant on funding and infrastructure and will require trained professionals to implement it. Having said that, it exemplifies early resolution behaviours, which if rolled out in other areas of the community has the potential to bring about cultural change.

Referral of neighbours to the local neighbourhood mediation service

This type of referral generally happens through housing associations. The housing officer will identify that there is an ongoing dispute and refer both parties to mediation. Generally, the parties will be given the option of a pre-mediation meeting in which they will discuss and clarify for themselves the important issues, what they want from the situation and how they might address it including a discussion around the pros and cons of mediation.

Facilitated forums to address conflict in the community

Facilitated forums present potentially multiple benefits in starting the conversation about conflict within the community and exploring options to address it. These include:

- Providing a safe space to start a difficult conversation.
- Identifying key issues that people are facing in the community and in so doing provide an opportunity to express their feelings about those issues.
- Identifying influencers in the community who are motivated to resolve conflicts because the conflicts directly impact on their lives.
- Increasing awareness and building skills in conflict resolution.

Because this type of forum can start to open up old wounds and bring current issues to the surface, they need to be managed carefully:

- Actual and potential conflicts between those present need to be identified and supported immediately.
- Resources need to be in place to support the resolution of some of these issues including mediation and personal conflict coaching.
- Sessions need to provide individuals with early resolution skills that are light touch, easily applicable and demonstrable.
- Actions and next steps need to be identified and followed up on so delegates feel a sense of ownership and a starting point for resolution.

Implement dynamic resolution solutions

Once the key issues and influencers have been identified, it is important to ensure that follow up is actioned. This means that people become equipped to use resolution skills and are supported to do this. Cross-community training in line with the seven principles can be a sustainable way of doing this together with the introduction of personal conflict coaches and mediators similar to the workplace model outlined earlier. In this way not only do a number of individuals across the community gain the skills needed to resolve conflicts in their day-to-day lives but the conversation deepens across the community with respect to the presenting issues. Also, individuals start to adopt a common method of resolution in line with the seven principles that has the potential to turn around understandings, misunderstandings and conversations within the community.

Because communities are not necessarily organised entities, a learning exchange of personal conflict coaching and mediation skills together with peer support is one way of developing practice, providing support to individuals dealing with conflict daily on the ground. In this way, personal conflict coaches and mediators can feed back their experience but also draw on the experience of others.

CHAPTER 10
PRINCIPLE 6: WALK THE WALK – USING CONFLICT RESOLUTION TOOLS IN EVERYDAY LIFE

If we can resolve the little irritations, fears and challenges we have with the people we encounter on a day-to-day basis, we stand a chance of transforming those relationships. We may also avoid those irritations and challenges turning into long-term resentments. It is not an exaggeration to say that if we achieve that personally we become closer to being able to make peace in the world and create a different paradigm.

On this basis, it is critical for businesses and the people who work in them to be aware that our personal and corporate social responsibility starts with the level to which we take responsibility for our behaviour and conflicts at work and with the relationships we have with the people we engage with every day.

Walking the conflict resolution walk for individuals

As we set ourselves up as conflict resolution advocates and experts, we immediately come face to face with personal challenges. We cannot resolve other people's conflicts if we are unwilling to look at our part in the conflicts we experience in our own life. We are forced to connect with those conflicts when we empathise with others and if we don't we come across as 'preachy' and disingenuous. At the same time, acknowledging the conflicts in our own life can make us feel vulnerable if we cannot see a way through them or through our behaviour within them.

If we are to embark on becoming an agent for conflict resolution in any way we need to be willing to acknowledge the conflicts in our own life and be open to changing the way we respond and react to them. In so doing, we build our resilience and capacity to deal with difficult situations as well as becoming better placed to support others in conflict. When we start looking at our own challenges we generally come across the following stumbling blocks which come in the form of telling ourselves:

● I don't have conflicts in my own life.

● I have so much conflict in my own life I'm never going to be able to help other people.

Generally neither of these are ever true. If we think that we don't have conflict in our own life we are often trying to avoid it but other people around us will experience it and it is likely to surface when we least expect it. Equally, our vulnerability in our own conflicts and appreciation of how challenging they can be can be an asset in terms of our own knowledge, expertise and, crucially, capacity to empathise.

Case study

Anna and Belinda were sisters whose elderly parents were unwell and needed help with a number of aspects of their care. They had always been close but had chosen different paths in life. Anna had always spent more time with her parents than Belinda who had a senior management job in a multinational company.

Anna started calling Belinda every day to ask her to help and complained that Belinda was unhelpful. Anna sent Belinda email links of possible options of things to help their parents. Belinda made a policy of not responding to emails that were not clearly asking her to do something. She thought that Anna was making too much of a fuss about her parents and tended to not respond to Anna's calls because she was too busy and found that they got on better the less contact they had.

This carried on for a number of years with no great consequence. Eventually Anna and Belinda's parents died and they met at the house to talk about what needed to happen to organise probate. At the house Belinda noticed a pair of earrings that her mother had always promised her and asked Anna if she could take them. She was shocked when Anna who was usually very calm shouted at her and told her she was the most selfish, self-centred person she had ever met and she had never once made an effort to build bridges. This came as a huge shock to Belinda who was completely at a loss about how to deal with the situation and restore the relationship with her sister.

If we are too ashamed of the reaction to conflict we experience in our own life, we miss out on the opportunity to find help with those conflicts. We are also less able to support others resolve similar situations by virtue of the fact that we aren't prepared to address them in our own life.

Case study

Johnny was a successful banker who was married with three young children. He had managed big teams and had always been praised and respected for the way he ran those teams and treated the people with them. Johnny's wife had given up work since having their second child three years ago.

At his local church people often confided in Johnny and he always seemed happy and able to help. But when he was made redundant, Johnny started to lose confidence in himself. He was worried about how he was going to support his family and about what he was going to do with his life. Johnny spent a lot of time at home looking for a job. His wife got a job and Johnny took on more of the responsibilities around the house and with the children. However, he felt resentful that his wife could go out and work and he found it hard to cope looking after the home every day. He started to have a lot of arguments with his wife and became very critical with the children.

Johnny started to wonder how, if he couldn't manage his own home life, he would be able to manage a team and go back to work. He felt like a fraud pretending to be a kind, capable person when in fact he felt like someone who couldn't even communicate or be loving with his own family. His shame started to take over to such a degree that he stopped applying for jobs for three months thinking that any employer would 'find him out' and realise that he was not the kind caring person he appeared to be. Johnny finally got a job 9 months later three of which had been wasted in not applying.

When Johnny did return to work he found that he was more able to relate to and support colleagues who had been on maternity and sick leave and were returning to work. He became a champion for diversity within the organisation. Johnny's strength was to acknowledge his management capabilities and the value they brought while at the same time accept that he had limitations and vulnerabilities. He found that when he started helping other people with their conflict situations in the knowledge that he struggled with these situations too, he began to learn from the support he provided and apply techniques that he used on or recommended to others in his personal life.

The CAN inventory

The CAN inventory provides a quick, personal check that we can run through daily to raise our Consciousness about the conflicts in our lives, Acknowledge them as potential triggers for change and growth and Now take action.

When we use the CAN inventory, we shine a light on those issues that we may prefer to brush over. Some people may question why we need to do that. Is that not turning something that was not a problem into a problem? The opposite is true, where we can tidy up the rough edges and resentments from our day, we can move through them and put them to bed. If we do not, they are more likely to build and create a snowball of blockages in the way we interact with other people and sometimes in the way we feel about and talk to ourselves. We become influenced in our decision-making without even knowing it and can therefore end up making poor decisions at work as a result of something going on at home.

Consciousness

Raising our consciousness involves us acknowledging and accepting that a fear (or a situation we have with someone else) exists and is disturbing us in some way. This stage does not require us to do anything about that situation other than accept its existence. We become more awake to it and its potential consequences and subsequently more alive to our part in it and what we might need to do about that.

Acknowledge

When we acknowledge the conflict as a potential trigger for change, we move into the mindset that this situation may lead us to a better place and that something good might come out of it. The reality is that when we make mistakes, our first response is not to celebrate them. Equally, when someone upsets us we are not inclined to thank them. However, if we can, we give ourselves an opportunity to change the dynamic, bring a lightness to the situation and often ensure that we do not find ourselves in the same situation again.

Now

The now in the taking action step emphasises that we must move on from simply acknowledging to being immediately willing to do something practical. We don't need to take that action straightaway, rather we need to be willing to set those actions in gear.

Taking action is often the first thing we want to do before raising our consciousness and acknowledging the opportunities within the conflict. But it is more than likely that this action is going to be a reaction that feels slightly out of our control if we have not fully thought it through. Taking time with these actions can be much more powerful. For example, try to wait three days before responding to someone who has upset you before talking about it. In general, when we do this, we come from a much more empowered place and are better able to communicate our position, wants, needs and feelings.

Action can be interpreted in a number of ways. For example, I once heard someone say that meditation is the action of sitting still. Equally, action may include asking for help. The more we take time to take action, the wider our options start to become. The action does not always require us to speak to or engage with the other person – rather we might need to work on resolving it within ourselves. Finally, if we are thinking about taking action with respect to the other person, we should identify whether we need to take that action now, later or at all.

Raise Consciousness		Acknowledge the conflict as a trigger for change			Now take action		
Who upset me/ What am I afraid of?	What happened?	Has anything like this happened to me before?	Could I have done anything differently?	Is this affecting my thoughts or behaviours in other areas?	Do I need help and how do I get it?	What do I need to do for myself?	Do I need to take action with respect to the other person? Now? Later? At all?

Walking the conflict resolution walk for businesses

As a business leader, 'walking the walk' might involve engaging with initiatives that are taking place within the community and supporting the development of early resolution skills as tools for leadership and management within the organisation.

When businesses engage with the community, they have more of an understanding of what goes on within it, and in turn communities find in local businesses a more accessible set of individuals than they had previously realised. This can start by businesses getting involved in initiatives that involve skills exchange where both members of the community and the businesses are valued for what they bring to the table. These initiatives almost have to start as an experiment. We never know how people are going to respond to each other in these situations, but where our starting point is a perspective of finding the win–win in these relationships there is a great deal of potential to build.

Case study

We trained a group of young people in early resolution skills and then took them into a corporate environment to demonstrate those skills. One would initially expect that the senior managers already had these skills. However, they were the first to admit that the listening techniques that the young people had demonstrated were different to the techniques that they used and gave them the opportunity to listen to and empathise with their clients and colleagues in a different way.

The process also allowed the senior managers to learn about the conflicts that young people were experiencing in the local community and enabled them to start thinking about how they could support the young people through work placements. This learning exchange was a forum for highly educated individuals to learn specific skills from local young people and those young people to be exposed to opportunities. The forum's existence in and of itself immediately dissolved the feeling of 'them and us' and provided the opportunity to build community cohesion across groups that may not have previously come into contact with each other, deeper mutual understanding and opportunities for business and community growth.

CHAPTER 11
PRINCIPLE 7: ENGAGE THE SAFETY NET – WHAT TO DO WHEN INFORMAL CONFLICT RESOLUTION DOESN'T WORK

There will be times when informal conflict resolution does not bring a resolution and at this point it will be important to re-evaluate the situation and options available. At the beginning of this book, we looked at the alternative options available. It will be important to consider these options in more detail and how and when best to employ them according to the situation.

It may be that there are large amounts of money or principles at stake. It may also be that a decision needs to be made by a professional or a higher authority to resolve or conclude the matter. Alternatively, tensions may be running so high that parties do not feel that they can engage with each other constructively and need a third way.

When it becomes clear that informal resolution is not working, there are a number of issues you need to consider.

Clarify your legal position

Good clear legal advice will help to form the basis of the choices you make. A legal adviser can never be expected to tell you if you are going to win or lose the case. This is because there are all sorts of details including what the other side's position and evidence is. We may have a strong moral position but this position may have no grounding in law. Equally, our legal position may start off as being strong until it is discovered, for example, that we unknowingly carried out illegal activities during the course of our employment which then deeply affects our credibility.

It can be helpful to get a broad brush picture of what might be done to resolve the issue with a professional view on whether from a legal perspective it will be in our interests to pursue the case.

Consider obtaining other expert advice

Often experts can help to clarify issues that avoid unnecessary future wrangling. For example, in a boundary dispute, a surveyor may clarify where the boundary is and what could be done about clarifying that, such as putting in steel tacks to clarify the boundary limits. In a building dispute, the surveyor may be able to give an opinion on whether the design and build was in line with current building regulations. Or in a dispute over the value of a business, a jointly appointed forensic accountant could give a valuation.

Sometimes expert advice is disputed between the parties, but at other times the parties can use that advice to take a sanguine view of their case or reach a compromise that can work for them. Lawyers will often bring in expert advice but it is helpful to be aware of the option before as well as during legal proceedings.

Clarify your business priorities

In some cases your legal position may be unclear, but from a commercial perspective, you may consider that taking a more aggressive approach through litigation may clarify that you are serious about your position. You may also evaluate that it is worth displaying that you are willing to fight to achieve your goal and to take the risk in the hope that the other side might be less confident of taking the risk.

You may also decide to litigate in the first instance as a show of force with a view to mediating at a later stage. Equally, you may consider that it is worth not doing anything about the situation and making compromises for the sake of the reputation of the business, potential loss of opportunity and similar considerations.

You may find it useful to list your own business priorities.

_____

_____

_____

Clarify your financial priorities

Your financial priorities will include whether you can afford to pursue the case and lose and whether, if you win the case, the other person will be able to compensate you. You may want to consider your approach to risk (low, medium or high) and consider legal action as an investment decision in this way. When considering financial priorities, it is important to take into account the amount of time that may be taken away from income-generating activities where we own or run the business or the knock-on effect of pursuing a claim on your job or business.

You may find it useful to list your own financial priorities.

_____

_____

_____

Clarify your personal priorities

We often think we know what our priorities are instinctively, but not taking the time to write them down can sometimes lead us to reactive decision-making. When we list our personal priorities, we help clarify them for ourselves and take them seriously in the decision-making process before rather than after the event.

These will include whether you have the time and emotional energy to pursue the case, how long it will take and how it will affect you and the people around you. It may be that bringing the other person to justice is very important to you in terms of valuing or standing up for yourself and aggressively pursuing a claim. Or you may feel strongly about the issue but need to find an option that does not compromise your mental or physical health or risk family tensions or potential breakdown in marital relationships.

It may be helpful to ask those closest around you what they think and talk through the potential effects on them so that expectations are also set with the people around you with respect to what you are letting yourselves in for and why. This is not only in order to make the decision in the first place but to ensure that you are fully equipped and prepared to follow the decision through later down the line.

If expectations are set up at the beginning and all those involved are bought into the process, the potential gain and the potential sacrifice, these relationships can be preserved and become stronger through the process.

You may find it useful to list your top three personal priorities.

_____

_____

_____

Write down what is most likely to make the situation better or worse.

This question is very difficult to answer, but it is worth bearing in mind that many conflicts start off being about one thing and morph into being about another.

List anything that you could do to make the situation better.

_____

_____

_____

List anything that you might do to make the situation worse

_____

_____

_____

In these circumstances, individuals have to be mindful of safeguarding their rights, keeping their options open and avoiding being heavily compromised.

As we engage in formal processes, we necessarily escalate the situation and, unless there is any process for de-escalation in place, the matter is likely to continue to entrench the parties in their positions against each other and solidify the conflict. In these situations, the tensions between the parties increase and additional grounds for conflict can very easily and quickly arise.

Case study

Joanna and Bill had an ongoing dispute with their neighbours Freda and Duncan about where the boundaries between their properties lay. They called in a surveyor to delineate boundary lines, but the surveyor was busy and took a while to visit the property and deliver the report. In the meantime, Joanna and Bill installed CCTV on their property to ascertain when Freda and Duncan were breaching their boundary by parking their car in a certain place.

Through that CCTV, Joanna and Bill realised that Freda was carrying out her coaching charity from the premises which was in breach of the restrictive covenants. Bill confronted Duncan about this outside their house and Duncan ended up pushing Bill and ordering him off the property. This incident resulted in the police getting involved and Duncan put in a further claim for harassment. Also, every encounter between the homeowners aggravated the situation and neither of them felt safe coming home at night.

Consider mediation

Very broadly, we can define civil, commercial or employment mediation as mediation that will take place as a precursor to or in the course of court or tribunal processes. The process is still relatively informal and fluid but provides an opportunity to find a strategic resolution to the presenting issues including those of fact and law. It also applies the principles in the context of legal processes.

Understanding the basics

When you are thinking about going to court, you will be encouraged to consider mediation. Civil and commercial mediation are terms used to describe the mediation process where the disagreement between individuals (civil) or between companies (commercial) may or is going to court or tribunal. The mediation will take place in the context of the legal process and will therefore be more formal. For example, people often use lawyers to set up this kind of mediation and to represent their legal interests in it.

If you are in a dispute with your employer or employee and that is likely to involve a termination of the working relationship, you might consider employment mediation. This may also happen if a workplace mediation has taken place to try and resolve the working issues between the parties but, for example, one of the parties has chosen to leave the organisation as a result and a follow-up claim or negotiation is being considered or brought.

If a claim is being brought then you will also need to notify ACAS with a view to carrying out a conciliation. Conciliation is very similar to mediation but it is more directional – the conciliator will be invested in a resolution and drawing concessions from both parties as opposed to empowering the parties to find a third way through their own means. If the employment mediation does go ahead, it will generally involve a legal element and you should seek or take legal advice to understand your options, risks and opportunities.

Will the mediation remain confidential?

Confidentiality in a civil, commercial or employment mediation only applies to what is said by the parties to the mediator. However, this type of mediation, and conversations relating to it, will also be governed by an agreement that the proceedings are 'without prejudice'.

This means that what is said during the mediation, and therefore in the context of the parties making a genuine effort to settle the dispute, is not used against the party who has said it if the mediation is unsuccessful. However, bear in mind that once this information is made available, there is always a possibility that it could be used to the benefit of the other party in some way at a later stage.

Will the mediation be binding?

Any agreement reached during the course of a mediation will only be binding to the extent to which agreements generally are binding according to normal contractual rules. The parties may come to an agreement on the day and then breach that agreement, in which case they may end up in dispute over that second agreement which will be enforceable or otherwise to the extent that any agreement is enforceable.

How do I decide whether to mediate or not?

Most mediation providers are more than happy to have a confidential discussion with you about whether or not mediation may be a helpful process in your particular circumstances. This gives you an opportunity to talk through your situation with someone who is not involved but understands the mediation process and may point you in the direction of getting help and advice to support you in the course of mediating or in finding another solution.

For example, if the person you are in conflict with is not answering your calls or emails, it will be difficult to engage them in mediation and so that will probably not be the best option unless and until they have at least been engaged in a litigation process.

Or if you don't want to be put in a position where you are face to face with the other person, the mediator will discuss how that might be possible in the context of the mediation. As with all effective resolution processes, that confidential discussion will allow you to think about and come to a conclusion about what the best solution for you is in the circumstances.

PART 3
MAKING A SUCCESS OF CIVIL, COMMERCIAL OR EMPLOYMENT MEDIATION

CHAPTER 12
GETTING THE MEDIATION PROCESS OFF THE GROUND

Mediation is an opportunity to find a strategic resolution to the presenting issue and to continue to apply the principles. The more effectively we can apply them, the better the result of the mediation is likely to be. The key to success will be using the tools to think clearly and make good decisions.

It is impossible to provide an exhaustive list of matters that might be suitable for mediation but essentially these will be matters that do not require an absolute decision about a point of law to be made. Having said that, even when such a decision is required, mediation may be key to ensuring that people can live with and integrate that decision into their day-to-day lives and avoid future litigation.

We will focus here on matters in which court or tribunal action is contemplated or in progress including:

- Disputes over payment terms, fulfilment of contracts including non-payment, how the contract was carried out or whether there was a breach of contract, warranty or guarantee covenant.

- Building contracts where builders are asking for money and clients are requesting outstanding matters to be completed or an itemisation of work invoiced.

- Disputes between property owners, developers and neighbours ranging from disagreements about options and valuations to arguments between neighbours including trespass, harassment, excessive noise, breach of boundary line or wall or landlord and tenant disputes ranging from dilapidations to rental payments.

- Disputes between financial institutions and their clients or customers relating to trade or financial instruments, compliance and regulatory matters.

- Disputes between individuals and professionals or local/central government organisations including incidents where people have suffered injury, financial loss or some other damage.

- Disputes between employers and employees (or former employees) where employees are bringing claims of discrimination or unfair dismissal or where the employer is alleging that the employee has taken away clients where they had agreed not to.

There are a few ways that the mediation process might be set in motion depending on whether the parties have advisers or not and what stage in the legal process they have reached.

Moving to mediation without legal advice

If you do not have someone acting on your behalf there are a number of actions you should take.

Find a mediator or mediation provider

It is often helpful to provide the other person with a choice of mediators or mediation companies and to set out the costs that you have been quoted. You can find a list on the Ministry of Justice website (http://civilmediation.justice. gov.uk) with a standard set of fees for small claims, as well as a choice of registered mediators.

Providing information in as transparent a way as possible allows the other person to have some choice and ownership in the process and not feel pushed into it. As I have already mentioned, most mediators or mediation providers will have a confidential discussion with the parties to help them decide if mediation is for them or not. It is worth establishing if this is possible so that the other party has some ownership and power in the process.

Find a suitable venue

Some mediations can take place over the telephone. In other cases three rooms or more will be needed (one for each of the parties and the other for the mediator to bring the parties together as and where necessary). The mediator or mediation provider will be able to advise on this and may be able to organise it but there are generally costs associated with this.

Identify dates

It is useful to identify three or four dates as options that might work. Generally, once you have decided to go ahead with mediation, it is helpful for it to take place as soon as possible to avoid further escalation of the issues.

Invite the other person to mediate

The invitation can be very informal. It is worth marking it 'Without prejudice save as to costs'. 'Without prejudice' indicates that you are making a genuine attempt to resolve the situation without making any admission as to guilt. The phrase 'save as to costs' means that the decision not to mediate may have costs penalties for the other party.

Case study

Mrs James and Mrs Kenefick were in a dispute over a shared boundary. Mrs James invited Mrs Kenefick to mediate the matter in 2014 and Mrs Kenefick refused. A financial settlement with respect to the claim was reached in 2017 at which point Mrs James had incurred £80,000 of legal fees and costs and Mrs Kenefick had incurred £25,000 of her own fees and costs.

The court decided that Mrs Kenefick had to pay Mrs James' £50,000 in costs in addition to her own costs partly on the basis that the same settlement could have been reached by a mediated settlement in 2014.

A form of words for an invitation to mediate is set out below. You should note that sometimes this kind of letter also includes a threat that if mediation is not agreed to within a certain timeframe then the next step for the writer to take will be that the writer will take the matter to court. This has not been included below.

Without prejudice save as to costs

Dear []

Re: Our partnership dispute

Following our [discussion/correspondence], I would like to propose that we mediate the issues between us with a view to coming to a successful conclusion for both of us.

I have contacted [mediation provider] who I found through the Ministry of Justice website http://civilmediation. justice.gov.uk/. They have [given me a choice of three mediators, details of which are attached] [OR] [confirmed that they work within the court mediation scheme and will provide us with a mediator of their choice in accordance with that scheme]. They have told me that you can contact them independently to have a confidential discussion with them about how mediation might work and whether you might want to go ahead.

I understand that the costs would be £… plus VAT per party for a … hour mediation.

I am available for a mediation on …. Once you have decided whether or not you would like to mediate, do let me know if you can make any of those dates or let me have a selection that might work for you.

Kind regards

Moving to mediation with legal advice

When you take a case to legal advisers, they will undoubtedly advise you on the merits of the case and when, whether and how to take the next steps to mediation. Factors that they will consider will include:

- Are you likely to get a better settlement at mediation if certain parts of your case are investigated or proven at an early stage?

- Is it better to start the litigation process in order to demonstrate you have a strong hand and mean business.
- Are you likely to win at court?
- Is the cost of pursuing the claim likely to exceed the value of the claim?

I have never met a lawyer who advises their client that they have more than a 70% likelihood of winning at trial, and so in this sense litigation is always a gamble. Having said that, most lawyers who think that their client has a good chance of success will do their best to pursue the claim and equip them at each stage with strategic as well as legal advice.

When working with lawyers, the most important thing to do is to take responsibility for your decisions and priorities and put your legal advice in that context. If you don't, you risk underestimating the costs of pursuing the matter including the other party's costs if you are unsuccessful.

Case study

Joseph was in a shareholder dispute with Will. Joseph had pursued the claim while Will had not appointed solicitors until late in the process in an effort to save costs. Joseph's solicitors had originally proposed mediation but Will refused as he thought they were bullying him and that he had a much better case.

Will appointed solicitors as the matter neared what was going to be a five-day trial. Will's advisers had told him he had a very good case and put his chances of success at 70%. He had incurred £20,000 costs and was likely to incur another £60,000 up until the trial which his lawyers had advised him he was not likely to recover. Joseph had incurred £100,000 and was likely to incur another £35,000 for the trial.

At mediation, they came to a number of agreements about what should be done next with the business and saw a way through to being able to work with each other albeit at arm's length, but Joseph was insisting on Will paying him £70,000 worth of costs. Because Will had thought Joseph had been unreasonable, he was incensed at this. However, he realised that he was placing himself at great risk putting the award of costs in the hands of the judge and decided instead to pay £50,000 in costs to Joseph.

Alternatively, we might regret the effect that we have had on the other party and on our own lives and business when we are successful.

Case study

Andrew was the co-director of a medium-sized, growing app development company. One of the employees brought a claim against his co-director, Melvin, for sexual harassment and against the company for breach of contract, which they decided to vigorously defend.

During the course of proceedings, Andrew was approached by another company with a view to that company buying them. However, the prospective purchaser was put off by the proceedings in progress and particularly concerned about the sort of claim that had been brought against the company.

In the end the company successfully defended the claim. However, Andrew found it distressing to see the employee at tribunal and the mental distress that she was obviously going through which exacerbated proceedings. Following the claim, there were further tacit rumours about Melvin's behaviour and Andrew felt that the trust that had previously existed in the company and with employees had been significantly eroded which made the job of getting things done and generating motivation and enthusiasm for the future within the business much harder.

CHAPTER 13
PREPARING FOR MEDIATION

Mediation is quite a fluid process and most mediators will tell you that no one mediation is the same. However, there are a number of common practices and themes that will run through a mediation that can be helpful to bear in mind.

Essentially, mediation is a process managed by the mediator. They will listen to preferences of advisers and clients as to what happens when, but essentially they will run the process with the objective of serving both parties optimally and take decisions with respect to that process accordingly. In terms of what is talked about and what is prioritised, this may be largely directed by the parties and their advisers, but when and how they are discussed will be managed by the mediator.

In this context, the mediation process in a civil, commercial or employment mediation will generally run as follows.

The pre-mediation

In the pre-mediation, the mediator will have a brief conversation with the parties and their advisers about the key issues for them. As well as that, the parties and the mediator will consider getting the right people around the table to enable effective decision making and the potential for sustainable agreement if reached.

In order to get the best out of the mediation, decisions need to be capable of being made on the day of the mediation meeting. For example, if a business partner is key to making the final decision then it may be that they need to be at the mediation or at least on the end of the phone. Equally, if the board needs to agree a settlement range, that will need to be done prior to the mediation and the flexibility or otherwise of that range will need to be discussed.

Most mediations will throw up factors that have not been previously thought of and so being able to have the flexibility to consult with key individuals during the course of the mediation process can significantly improve the outcome.

Discussions will need to be had as to the type or level of legal representation ranging from whether to have a full team of barristers and solicitors around the table to having a legal adviser at the end of the telephone or not at all.

Finally, the parties may want to consider if family members or close friends can or should attend. This can be crucial in making a decision that might affect the whole family, but at the same time parties need to be sensitive about this as it might create unnecessary antagonism or diversions.

<u>Preparing fully</u>

The better prepared the parties are for a mediation, the more efficient and effective the process will be and the less room there is for surprises. The questions set out below are aimed at supporting the parties to ensure that their preparation is focussed and effective:

List the key documents that are relevant below or in a separate document including court documents, witness statements and key correspondence. If lawyers are involved, both parties will agree these documents and send them to the mediator.

_____

_____

_____

What are the main positions and arguments from your perspective and the other party's perspective? Try and rank them strongest to weakest.

	Your position / arguments	Their position / arguments
Liability		
Value of the claim / counterclaim		
Liability for costs		

_____

_____

_____

_____

List costs incurred and anticipated future costs and the effect legal aid or insurance could have on those costs.

	You	Other party
Costs to date		
Costs to trial		
Likely amount of costs recoverable at assessment		
Impact of insurance		
Impact of legal aid		

What are the consequences for you of not resolving the matter?

_____

_____

_____

What are the consequences for them of not resolving the matter?

_____

_____

_____

What are the options as you see them for resolution?

_____

_____

_____

What are the potential opportunities that could come out of this situation? (Include even those situations you don't think are likely.)

_____

_____

_____

The civil, commercial or employment mediation session

The mediator will generally arrange for the parties to arrive separately and settle into their rooms. The mediator will then take some time with the parties and, if appropriate, their advisers and work out the best way of running the day. This may be to bring the parties together for a joint meeting, to have a series of separate meetings in which the mediator is shuttling between and rooms, or to bring the advisers and experts together.

Establish the issues and principles

The mediator will support the parties to establish the issues and principles.

Even when litigation is in process and issues have been highly organised, when we are involved in conflict, numerous issues can become confused. The mediator helps the parties separate out the relevant from the less relevant issues in terms of the priorities that have been defined for the session. They will also help the parties to work out for themselves what they do or do not wish to disclose to the other party.

The mediator will spend time with the parties separately and together to establish what is at issue. A point of principle for one party can often seem irrelevant to another but it can also be a deal maker or breaker. It is therefore crucial to ensure that issues which may not be important on the surface, but are significant for the parties, are considered and prioritised by the mediator and the parties.

The mediator will then work out whether to address the issues in private meetings with the parties or in joint meetings and the best point to address them. In this way, the parties are much more likely to be able to walk away from the mediation with a clean slate having covered all the bases.

Explore the issues

Once the mediator has established clarity with the parties about what is and is not at issue, they will give the parties an opportunity to reflect and, if necessary, vent about those issues and then help the parties to prioritise them and narrow them down.

Negotiate and develop options

Once the parties have established the big picture issues, the mediator will start to drill down on the potential and actual areas on which the parties agree, the areas on which they disagree and areas in which there is or may be room for movement.

At this point it will be important for the parties to be as open as possible with the mediator as to the flexibility or otherwise existing within those negotiation parameters so that the mediator has the fullest picture of what may and may not be possible. The mediator will then work with the parties and their advisers to negotiate the issues with the aim of achieving optimum success for all the parties.

Make decisions

When the final positions of all the parties have been reached, they will know if they are willing or ready to come to an agreement on some or all of the issues. If they are, the mediator will work with the parties to ensure that the agreement is SMART: Specific, Measurable, Achievable, Realistic and Time Bound.

Most important is that these decisions are decisions that the parties can live with. Mediation is a unique moment during the proceedings in which parties have an opportunity to see the big picture and take time to think about their options. After the mediation, that opportunity, and sometimes even progress made on agreeing points and bringing people together, may be lost. Having said that, the potential sustainability of the agreement is crucial and to ensure this is the case, even when the decisions have been made, the mediator may test the parties rigorously on their commitment to those decisions to ensure that the agreement will last.

Case study

When I was working on a neighbourhood dispute, I worked with neighbours who had originally been friends but had fallen out over noise issues between the flats and hadn't spoken to each other for a great length of time. At the end of the mediation they came to an agreement about how they would be able to live together in the future.

I happened to walk past the bus stop after the mediation and saw them standing next to each other talking to each other calmly and sharing a joke. From my perspective as a mediator, this was an indication that the agreement they had reached had a chance of being sustainable.

Close and follow-up

A number of things can happen during and after the mediation session and so a mediator's mantra is always 'expect the unexpected' particularly when personality issues are a component part of the conflict. Because of this, the agreement reached needs to be as comprehensive as possible and should cover what happens if things do not work out as expected.

For example, neighbours may agree to formally abide by certain boundaries – to keep out of each other's way – but they will also need to consider what to do if they need to talk to each other in the event of say a tree falling from one property to another.

In some cases, the mediator may follow up with the parties after the mediation session to smooth over some challenges in sustaining the agreement or agree some finer communication points. The mediator may also support the parties to come to terms with circumstances post-agreement and find a way to move forward.

CHAPTER 14
BECOMING A MEDIATOR

Often when people experience mediation or undergo some related training, they are inspired by the approach and start to think about becoming a mediator themselves. I knew when I started my neighbourhood mediation course (when most people thought I was talking about meditation) that this was something I wanted to do full-time. And it turned out to be a long road to build a practice in the field of civil, commercial, employment and workplace mediation.

As mediation is a relatively young profession, there are a number of issues to consider. For some, being a mediator and conflict resolution specialist will become a full-time job. For others, undergoing mediation training and understanding fully how mediation works will support their professional practice. And for others it will simply be a management tool to pick up as and when required.

Training as a mediator

There are a number of options to train as a mediator based on the type of mediation you will carry out such as civil and commercial, employment, workplace and neighbourhood. There will be a distinction between training for the purposes of supporting parties who are in the process of an actual or potential court based dispute and one that involves the potential preservation or a working or living relationship.

Both practices and sets of skills cross over but the emphasis will be different. For example, the principal expertise of a civil and commercial mediator may not necessarily be in building dialogue between the parties and the expertise of a workplace mediator will not be in negotiating a financial settlement. Once you have trained in one area, you can always expand your practice into other areas. When starting off though, think about where you might be able to practise your skills and where your clients may come from.

Getting experience and ongoing support

Once you have been classroom-trained, you will need to get experience of how mediation works in practice before going out into the field on your own. It is useful to see a variety of mediators at work by assisting them on their cases and by seeing potential challenges that come up in practice. Most civil and commercial mediators are more than happy for you to shadow or assist them, subject to their clients being happy.

In the case of a workplace or neighbourhood mediation, a 'co-mediation' in which the mediators of two parties meet together can work very well and provide a great foundation and experience. In both cases, you will need to take your lead from the more experienced mediator.

Essential to ongoing continuing professional development as a mediator will be debriefing with other mediators and reviewing your practice. Key questions mediators will ask themselves after a mediation are:

- What were the key stages in the mediation?
- What techniques were particularly helpful?
- What were the turning points?
- What might you do differently?
- What skills would you like to work on?
- What can you do to improve those skills?

It is important to review your analysis of the mediation with another mediator to get their perspective of how you managed the process and your evaluation of it. For example, we could sometimes do things differently but that change may not alter the outcome or it may have created a new challenge or problem. Another person's perspective allows us to be clear about our practice, learn from it and move on. It also helps us to continually remind ourselves as mediators that the outcome is always the choice of the parties, and what we might think in retrospect could have been the right or better result may only be our perception and may be wrong.

In organisations where there are a number of mediators, practice review can be a good opportunity for learning and development as well as a regulator of good practice. It may also bring up themes of management practice within the organisation that can be fed back in a way that is anonymous and confidential.

Building your practice

Key to building a mediation practice will be building on interventions that help and work. This does not mean that you have to be mediating all the time to begin with but instead applying the principles and mediation techniques to situations you come across, to be practising a mediation mindset whenever you can and demonstrating the effectiveness of the approach which then builds trust in the mediation process.

Practice and experience are vital to building confidence and obtaining a broad experience of conflict situations and where they, and the mediation process, can potentially come undone.

As with building any business, the reality is that this will be as much about who you know as what you know. Many people choose mediators with experience in a certain field, so if you work in a certain area already it is helpful to focus on that and build your practice around it.

Perception can be very powerful. Many people perceive that you need to be a subject specialist to mediate in that area. The reality is that although you need to understand the concepts at play, you do not have to be the expert. Rather, you will need to manage the experts and expertise and keep your own opinions and therefore ego out of the equation. Having said that, if your clients feel more comforted that you have a background in a certain area, you will have their confidence to run the process and that confidence will be key to helping them achieve the result they need.

Building your practice will require you to educate other people to help them understand the benefits that the process will bring to them and, indeed, their careers. It will also be about building on your education and expertise as a mediator and constantly digging into your own personal and professional challenges through conflict.

If you are working in a certain field, it is useful to build on the expertise and contacts you have developing those relationships and communicating the benefits of mediation as it applies to the field. Identify the strategic alliances that you can make with people to help them do what they are already doing better. By working in this way, people can start to identify you as an industry expert in that field, a reputation you will then be able to build on.

There is no doubt that working in the area of conflict resolution and empowering others to get to the other side of otherwise difficult conversations and negotiations is extremely fulfilling. It is also a great responsibility which is lightened by ensuring that we are always lead by the following guiding principles:

- Be aware of your impulses to fix and know that they are unlikely to provide the most helpful answers;
- Always remember that the most comprehensive solution always lies with the parties and they are capable of achieving it if they want to;
- Mediators are never higher authorities but rather trusted servants;
- Not everyone wants to resolve their conflicts now, later or ever;
- Take every opportunity to learn and transform through your own conflicts;
- Ask for help and be prepared to give the help you received.

APPENDICES

APPENDIX 1: EMPLOYEE QUESTIONNAIRE

Thank you for participating in this questionnaire. Its aim is to gauge your personal experiences of conflict within the organisation. It is based on the premise that conflict is a normal part of our everyday work life and can range from a difference of opinion to total communication breakdown.

Some of the answers may seem obvious to you. Please answer them anyway. Once we have collated all the results of the questionnaire, we will be thinking about what we can do to transform our conflicts into opportunities for learning and growth so your input is invaluable in this process. If you want to know more, you can contact [].

The contents of this questionnaire are necessarily completely CONFIDENTIAL and we appreciate your total candidness.

You can tick more than one box in each section.

1. Do you have a FORMAL process to deal with disagreements and conflicts within your organisation?

☐ Yes

☐ No

☐ I don't know

2 Do you have an INFORMAL process to deal with disagreements or conflicts within your organisation?

☐ Yes

☐ No

☐ I don't know

3 If you have an INFORMAL process to deal with disagreements or conflicts within your organisation, write down briefly your understanding of how it works.

_____

_____

_____

4 Where you have been in a difficult situation with someone at work, did you:

☐ Resolve the problem with the person in question directly

☐ Obtain support from another person within the organisation to resolve the problem

☐ Remain silent

☐ Seek revenge / retaliation

☐ Talk to the person in question

☐ Talk to the HR department

☐ Raise a grievance

☐ Talk to a lawyer / in-house legal team

☐ Talk to your union rep

☐ Talk to ACAS

☐ Take sickness leave

☐ Consider taking sickness leave

5 Have you experienced any of the following during the course of working for the organisation?

☐ Feeling undermined

❑ Being unable to carry out your job because of another person
❑ Being unable/unwilling to talk to colleagues
❑ A severe problem with a colleague
❑ None of the above

6 If you have experienced any of the issues set out in 5 above, please detail as far as possible what happened and how it affected you.

_____

_____

_____

_____

7 Where you have been in a difficult situation or conflict with another person at work, do you feel that it was resolved successfully for you? Please explain your answer.

_____

_____

_____

_____

8 Where you have been in a difficult situation or conflict with another person at work, do you feel that the other person felt that it was resolved successfully for them? Please explain your answer.

_____

_____

_____

_____

9 Have you ever withheld information from your boss or co-worker (e.g. buried bad news) in order to avoid an argument?

❑ Yes
❑ No

10 In your opinion, why do disagreements in your workplace come about?

❑ Lack of communication
❑ Ineffective communication (if so, please describe below e.g. shouting, nobody talking to each other etc.)
❑ Other (please describe)

_____

_____

11 Which of the following most accurately describes the approach your boss takes to address internal conflicts?

☐ Collaborative (e.g. joint working / problem solving)
☐ Accommodating (e.g. agreement with some element of sacrifice or resentment)
☐ Avoidant (e.g. walking away)
☐ Aggressive (e.g. shouting or threatening)
☐ Compromising (e.g. demonstrating elements of give and take)

12 Where you have been in a conflict situation at work, did you

☐ Increase the effort you put into the job
☐ Decrease the effort you put into the job
☐ Put the same amount of effort into the job
☐ Lose work time worrying about it
☐ Lose sleep worrying about it

13 If you decided to leave the organisation, what would be your main reason for doing so? (Please be specific so if, for example, the reason is stress, then identify the cause of the stress)

_____

_____

14 If you have experienced a conflict at work, how comfortable did you feel about confiding in your boss about the issue?

☐ Very comfortable
☐ Fairly comfortable
☐ Not comfortable at all
☐ Not applicable

15 If you have experienced a conflict at work, how comfortable did you feel about confiding in HR about the issue?

☐ Very comfortable
☐ Fairly comfortable
☐ Not comfortable at all
☐ Not applicable

If you experienced a conflict at work who, if anyone, did you talk to about the issue?

_____

_____

APPENDIX 2: DIRECTOR/TEAM LEAD QUESTIONNAIRE

Thank you for participating in this questionnaire. Its aim is to gauge your personal experiences of conflict within the organisation. It is based on the premise that conflict is a normal part of our everyday work life and can range from a difference of opinion to total communication breakdown.

The questionnaire is put together in two sections, to establish the quality of interactions within the organisation and the effects of those interactions on you.

The contents of this questionnaire are necessarily completely CONFIDENTIAL and we appreciate your total candidness.

Some of the answers may seem obvious to you. Please answer them anyway.

Once we have collated all the results of the questionnaire, we will be thinking about what we can do to transform our conflicts into opportunities for learning and growth so your input is invaluable in this process. If you want to know more, you can contact [].

You can tick more than one box in each section.

1 On average, how many days of your time have been spent on grievances, disciplinary hearings or employee-related court/tribunal proceedings during the course of the last financial year?

☐ O
☐ 1–5
☐ 6–10
☐ 11–12
☐ 20+

If above 20, please specify how many:

2 For the purposes of quantifying the true cost of conflicts, please detail your annual gross salary.

☐ £0–40,000
☐ £40–80,000
☐ £80,001 – 120,000
☐ £120,001 – 160,000
☐ £160,001 – 2000,000
☐ £200,001 +

3 In your opinion, has the running of the business been compromised by internal disagreements or conflicts? If so, how?

_____
_____
_____
_____

4 Do you think your organisation has lost or could lose money as a result of internal conflicts? If so, how?

_____
_____
_____
_____

5 Do you think that the future of your organisation could be compromised by internal conflicts?

☐ Yes
☐ No

6 If your answer to question 5 above is YES, please explain how.

_____

_____

_____

_____

7 Have you ever referred conflicts to HR?

☐ Yes
☐ No

8 If your answer to 7 above is NO, why not?

_____

_____

_____

_____

9 If your answer to 7 above is YES, how successful / unsuccessful was the intervention. Please explain your answer.

_____

_____

_____

APPENDIX 3: HEAD OF LEGAL/HR/FINANCE QUESTIONNAIRE

Thank you for participating in this questionnaire. Its aim is to gauge your personal experiences of conflict within the organisation. It is based on the premise that conflict is a normal part of our everyday work life and can range from a difference of opinion to total communication breakdown.

The questionnaire is put together in two sections, to establish the quality of interactions within the organisation and the effects of those interactions from your perspective.

The contents of this questionnaire are necessarily completely CONFIDENTIAL and we appreciate your total candidness.

Some of the answers may seem obvious to you. Please answer them anyway.

Once we have collated all the results of the questionnaire, we will be thinking about what we can do to transform our conflicts into opportunities for learning and growth so your input is invaluable in this process. If you want to know more, you can contact [].

You can tick more than one box in each section.

1 How many grievances were raised in your organisation during the course of the last year (please specify whether it was in the last financial or calendar year by ticking the box)?

☐ 0
☐ 1–5
☐ 6–10
☐ 11–20
☐ 21–30
☐ 31–40
☐ 41–50
☐ 50+

Financial year ☐
Calendar year ☐

If above 50, please specify how many _____

2 Please detail below the number and types of grievances raised.

	0	1–5	6–10	11–20	20+
Bullying/ harassment					
Racial discrimination					
Sexual discrimination					
Equal pay					
Constructive dismissal					
Other					

3 Please detail in how many cases the following stages were reached in the grievance process.

	O	1–5	6–10	11–20	20+
Grievance resolved informally					
Formal meeting held to discuss the grievance					
Referral to independent third party (excluding mediation)					
Mediation					
Appeal					
Tribunal					

4 How many disciplinary proceedings were started during the course of the last year (please specify whether it was in the last financial or calendar year by ticking the box)?

- ☐ O
- ☐ 1–5
- ☐ 6–10
- ☐ 11–20
- ☐ 21–30
- ☐ 31–40
- ☐ 41–50
- ☐ 50+

   If above 50 please specify how many _____

- ☐ Financial year
- ☐ Calendar year

5 Please set out below, in how many cases the following stages were reached in the disciplinary process

	O	1–5	6–10	11–20	20+
Matter resolved informally					
Formal meeting held to discuss the matter					
Referral to independent third party (excluding mediation)					
Mediation					
Appeal					
Tribunal					

6 How much was spent on external legal fees relating to employee grievances or disciplinaries during the course of the last year (please specify whether it was the last financial or calendar year in the boxes below)?

- ☐ £0–5,000
- ☐ 5,000 – 10,000
- ☐ £10,001 – 20,000
- ☐ £20,001 – 50,000
- ☐ £50,001 – 100,000
- ☐ £100,001 – 250,000
- ☐ £250,000 plus please specify _____
- ☐ Financial year
- ☐ Calendar year

7 How much was spent on financial settlements relating to employee grievances or disciplinaries during the course of the last year (please specify whether it was the last financial or calendar year in the boxes below)?

- ☐ £0–5,000
- ☐ £5,000 – 10,000
- ☐ £10,001 – 20,000
- ☐ £20,001 – 50,000
- ☐ £50,001 – 100,000
- ☐ £100,001 – 250,000
- ☐ £250,000 plus please specify _____
- ☐ Financial year
- ☐ Calendar year

8 Think of a typical case you have been involved in. How many hours or days of management time were spent on internal discussions (e.g. HR – Manager), board briefings, staff interviews and calls or meetings with lawyers?

_____

_____

_____

9 On the basis of your answer to question 8, calculate the cost of internal management time spent on this matter as follows:

Hourly rate of individual 1 (= salary / 365 / 8 x hours spent)

Hourly rate of individual 2 (= as above)

Hourly rate of individual 3 (= as above)

Hourly rate of individual 4 (= as above)

Hourly rate of individual 5 (= as above)

Total:

Multiply the total by the number of hours or days spent as above based on an eight hour day. What is the estimated cost of internal management time spent on a typical case?

_____

_____

10   Have employees taken sick days or gone on permanent sick leave as a result of a conflict or disagreement within the organisation?

☐ Yes

☐ No (Go directly to question 13)

☐ If your answer to 10 above is YES how many days were lost?

_____

_____

_____

_____

☐ If your answer to 10 above is YES what was the value of the man hours lost? (refer to question 9 for calculation method)

_____

_____

☐ In your opinion has the organisation been materially compromised by internal conflict. For example has it lost money or opportunities because of internal conflicts?

_____

_____

_____

☐ Have you witnessed a conflict in the organisation which has compromised its clients or stakeholders? If so, please summarise what happened and/or the risks and/or the consequences as you see them.

_____

_____

_____

APPENDIX 4: CLIENT/ STAKEHOLDER QUESTIONNAIRE

Thank you for participating in this questionnaire. We want to improve our relationships within and outside of [organisation name] and are focussing on how we manage conflict with our staff, clients and stakeholders.

We understand that conflict is a normal part of our everyday work life and can range from a difference of opinion to total communication breakdown. We want to use it as an opportunity to learn and grow.

The contents of this questionnaire are necessarily completely CONFIDENTIAL and we appreciate your total candidness. If there is anything specific you would like to raise with us please contact [].

Some of the answers may seem obvious to you. Please answer them anyway.

You can tick more than one box in each section.

1   How long have you done business with us?

☐   0–1 years

☐   1–3 years

☐   3+ years

2   Have you ever felt irritated, frustrated, angry or upset in communications with employees of [organisation's name]?

☐   Yes

☐   No

3   If the answer to 2 above is "YES", please explain why and/or what happened

_____

_____

_____

4   Do your communications with [organisation's name] result in you feeling more or less motivated to do more business with us?

☐   More

☐   Less

☐   Doesn't make a difference

5   Have you told other people if and when you have been unhappy about communications or your relationship with [organisation's name]?

_____

_____

_____

6   Have you ever NOT recommended us to your contacts because of how our people have communicated with you?

_____

_____

_____

_____

7   What could we change about the way we deal with disagreements or difficulties with you?

_____

_____

_____

_____

INDEX